Happy 40ᵗʰ

Kent
Tellers of Tales

by
Pat Davis

Geerings of Ashford Ltd.,
Ashford, Kent, England.

Kent
Tellers of Tales

Geerings of Ashford Ltd.,
Ashford, Kent, England

First published 1996

© Pat Davis

ISBN 1 873953 29 1

*Designed and printed by
Geerings of Ashford Ltd., Ashford, Kent, England.*

Contents

Dedication

THIS book is enthusiastically dedicated to my P. A., my long standing and long suffering wife, Pat.

Without her dynamic drive this book might never have been completed.

Thanks, Pat!

A Man of Rare Reticence . . .

THE
LAMENTA=
BLE AND TRVE TRA-
GEDIE OF M. AR-
DEN OF FEVERSHAM
IN KENT.

Who was moſt wickedlye murdered, by
the meanes of his diſloyall and wanton
wyfe, who for the loue ſhe bare to one
Moſbie, hyred two deſperat ruf-
fins Blackwill and Shakbag,
to kill him.

Wherin is ſhewed the great mal-
lice and diſcimulation of a wicked woman, the vnſatiable deſire of filthie luſt
and the ſhamefull end of all
murderers.

Jmprinted at London for Edward
White, dwelling at the lyttle North
dore of Paules Church at
the ſigne of the
Gun. 1592.

Surely a title-page to end all title-pages?

THERE was even skulduggery - though minor - between rival printers for this prize. Edward White, dwelling 'at the lyttle Northdore of St Paul's Church at the signe of The Gun' had pirated Abell Jeffe's 'Spanish Tragedy'. So Jeffe, tit-for-tat, pirated White's 'Master Arden'. And was sentenced by the Court of the Stationers' Company to have all his illegal copies 'confiscated and forfayted'.

The actual authorship of the play is much less clear. Amazingly the title page bore no name. So for four centuries there has been happy dispute between literary eggheads: Shakespeare . . . ? Kyd . . . ? Marlowe . . . ? They agreed 'it was good theatre, good poetry too. Indeed a bold experiment in the drama of the future'. Whole passages reminded many of Shakespeare but just as many averred the imagery was Marlowe's. Finally 20th century poet and novelist John Masefield 'settled' the issue: 'Arden bears no single trace of Shakespeare's mind' he sturdily maintained. And so peaceful Kent can justly claim this vile and bloody tragedy as its own.

Murder most foul - but do not waste your sympathy on Master Arden. He was no wronged paragon. Indeed, he was known in Faversham as a covetous man, 'a preferer of private gain rather than common good'. One who, for fear of losing profitable business, was prepared 'to wynke at his wife's lewdness'. Alice Arden was young, tall, and fair of face and figure; her lover, Mosbie, swart and black. She had 'lain with him carnally; fed him delicate meates; and bought him rich apparel'.

But if she was ever to marry Mosbie, Arden must die. And it was she who made the first move. She visited a Faversham artist, one Clarke, so skilled in poisons that he could paint a portrait upon which it was death to look. Fearful that it might be she who inadvertently looked, Alice settled for a simpler but equally deadly potion. In her eagerness she so over-seasoned her husband's potage that, sickened, he spat it out.

Thwarted but undeterred, Mistress Arden turned for help to a neighbour, Greene, who bitterly hated Arden for swindling him and for 'fetching him a great blow' in their dispute. In his turn, Greene, together with the honest goldsmith Bradshaw, journeyed to Shooter's Hill (where Shakespeare was to set Falstaff's lying tale of assault by desperate highwaymen). Here, ruthless vagabonds and soldiers returning from the wars were to be found - and bought.

And here, for 10 angels (£10) each, Greene hired Shakebag and Black Will. The latter, 'a terrible cruel ruffian', had, as a soldier in Boulogne, 'committed many heinous robberies'. And swore vilely with almost every word. This unholy pair bribed Arden's servant Michael as 'inside man'. Bribed him as Clarke had been bribed with the promise that, murder done, he should enjoy in marriage the ready charms of Susan, Mosbie's sister, Alice's serving maid!

These conspirators made no fewer than five attempts to murder Arden as he rode about his business. All failed - through bungling or mischance. Now Arden had to be murdered in his own home before his wife's very eyes. Not suspecting treachery, he gladly agreed to play 'three games of backgammon for a French crown' with Mosbie. Heard him utter the victor's customary challenge 'May I take you, Sir?'.

Innocent sounding enough. But it was the signal for Black Will to burst into the room, draw a cloth tight round Arden's neck and strangle him.

To make assurance doubly sure Mosbie 'struck him with a tailor's great pressing iron to the very Brayne' and then cut his throat with his dagger. Alice, not to be outdone, also struck with her own small dagger.

A thorough enough job - but a sorely botched one. The Mayor, alerted by Alice's feigned lamentations for a missing loved one, called out the Watch. And it was Prune, the grocer, who found Arden's body, with household rushes still sticking to it, dumped near the Abbey wall. Unerased footprints in the newly fallen snow led them straight to Arden's house - to bloodstains on the floor; on Mosbie's clothing; and on the knife which bungling Michael, with poor aim, had failed to throw down the well.

It was 'manyfestly well approved that he had been slayne in his own home'. All Alice's pleas and lies, that 'he had kept wicked company' and that he had ill-treated her . . . fell on deaf ears.

Justice was salutary and sweeping. Alice was burnt at Canterbury, 'all her flesh and bones to ashes turned'. Mosbie, and his unwitting sister, though not privy to the deed, died more quickly on the Smithfield gibbet. Greene and Michael both 'lost their breath' in the same crude way. Shakebag fled to Southwark - only to be killed in a drunken brawl there. Black Will escaped to Flushing - but not to safety for he too was apprehended and burnt. And even honest Bradshaw who had no hand in or knowledge of the murder, also died. Only Clarke disappeared into thin air - but then he was a dealer in magic and poison. And surely too it was magic that for two years no grass grew where Arden's body had touched the ground.

A rich melodrama, loved alike by 16th century groundlings and fops. And still 'enjoyed' today by more sophisticated audiences reared on 20th century T.V. violence.

Quotation:
'The people of Faversham have doubly murdered this play by excessive bad Manuscript copies and their more injudicious acting'.

BARHAM, Richard Harris (1788-1845)

Versifying vicar . . .

HAD he thought of it first, Barham, tongue in cheek, might well have said, 'The Law is a H'ass' when it let him slip through its fingers to take, not silk - but the cloth.

Richard was born at No 61 Burgate in the heart of Canterbury. His father, a-bottle-of-port-a-day man, prosperous hop farmer, and Alderman to boot, was a man of no small substance. Some 27 stones of it, to be precise! And he could, when he wished, as he often proudly did, trace his lineage back to the knight Randal Fitzurse, treacherous murderer of Archbishop Thomas à Becket in his own Cathedral. Considerably less aristocratic was his liaison with his housekeeper of which Richard was the by-product.

He was educated not locally at King's School but in London at St Paul's. When he was 14 the 'Dover Mail', obviously unaware of the importance of the young lad it was carrying, overturned outside the Bricklayer's Arms. More dead than alive, Richard was dragged along with it and his hand nearly severed. It was the High Master's wife who nursed him selflessly; saved his hand which over-eager surgeons threatened to amputate; and recognised his versifying ability.

Outgrowing his role of practical joker he became Head of School, and proceeded on his way to Brasenose College, Oxford, to study Law. There he teamed up with Theodore Hook, fellow versifier and joker. And still found time enough to gamble himself into a quagmire of debt. Desperate, he made a fervent appeal to his guardian, Lord Rokeby. Was turned down flat. A loan? 'Certainly not, Sir'. An outright gift? Why 'Yes' - together with sound advice on the perils and pitfalls of gambling.

Hardly the best of starts for someone with only a modest B.A. now intent on a career in the Church. But in 1813, he was ordained, and a wise bishop, for Kent's benefit, set him up as curate at Westwell, near Ashford. Sadly it was not for Barham's benefit. For there, in a parsonage 'damp and dilapidated' his first two sons died.

Four years later he was promoted to the living at Snargate (where even today sheep graze in the graveyard). Amid the mystery and the beauty of the Marsh which he dubbed 'The fifth quarter of the Globe', he enjoyed the life of a country curate. A curate who hospitably invited guests to dine - in verse:

> 'O Doctor, wilt thou dine with me
> And drive on Tuesday morning down?
> Can ribs of beef have charms for thee:
> The fat, the lean, the luscious brown?'

Amongst a country flock he numbered of course an unobtrusive score of Free Traders: a euphemism for smugglers which would have delighted

John Lyly. Jogging back from a late call, he not infrequently met them - vague figures in shadowy Marsh mist. But from these rough and ready men, some with pistol and cutlass, 'he received nothing of outrage or incivility' merely a quietly growled 'Tis only Passon'. And for his part he adopted a studiously averted gaze.

Their business was not his; nor his, theirs, except . . . Except when, with the Excisemen hard on their heels, tobacco might find temporary lodging in Snargate belfry, or Hollands in the deep shadows of the vestry table. Commodities both as much appreciated by squire and parson as by blacksmith and shepherd.

It was, literally and metaphorically, far more upsetting when, in 1819, he overturned his gig, broke one leg and sprained the other ankle. For weeks, mightily bored, he lay in bed. Such an 'impetus' was always necessary to set Barham's pen in motion. In this case, he knocked up a novel 'Baldwin' which, unhappily, in the printer's phrase, 'Fell dead from the press'. Rheumatism set in and he had time enough to half finish 'My Cousin Nicholas'.

Chance stepped in again to change his life. With a daughter seriously ill, he posted up to London to consult a specialist. And there in the bustle of the Strand he chanced on a friend, hurrying, letter in hand, to the post. It was a letter urging an acquaintance to apply for a vacancy as a Minor Canon of St Paul's. Need more be said? Barham did apply - in verse.

From Marsh to Metropolis. As always there was a balance sheet to be reckoned. On the debit side there was the loss of the Marsh, 'gooseberry wine, pears and codlings'. And tragically there was to be the death of three more children in London. On the credit side: installation as a Minor Canon in 1821; renewed friendship with fellow wit and eccentric Edward Cannon; Chaplaincy of the Vintners' Company; founder membership of the Garrick Club; and appointment as Priest-in-Ordinary to His Majesty's Chapel Royal. (A strange title perhaps for so extraordinary a man).

The need to help his old friend, Richard Bentley whose 'Miscellany', despite contributions from a certain Charles Dickens, was in danger of foundering, gave him another impetus. So did the enthusiastic wife of a full blown Canon Residentiary. She fed him titbits of old legends to bring back to life in rollicking verse. She even committed larceny when secretly she abstracted 'My Cousin Nicholas' from a cluttered drawer and posted it to 'Blackwood's'. Barham knew nothing at all of this until a magazine with his article in it - and a request for further articles - was pushed through his letterbox.

Barham, unfeignedly pious for all his joking, never neglected his spiritual duties. In particular he devoted much time to patching up fierce disputes between the old crones in his Mile End Road Almshouses: 'the twelve odalisques in his harem'. As a result he became the 'Slave of the Lamp' working by its light until 2 or 3 am.

Once in his stride there was no holding him. His imagination ran riot; his wit was honed sharper still; his verses swept on at a rollicking pace; and his rhymes were masterpieces of ingenuity. 'The Witches' Frolic' and 'The Blasphemer's Warning' macabre and slightly risqué, might not sound meet offerings from a Minor Canon. So he filched a name and 'the *Ingoldsby* Legends' were born into lively longevity. The first edition in 1840 was swept from the shelves by 'A Generous and Enlightened Public'.

Barham's range was wide . . . Nell was Cook by trade as well as name. And when her Canon, altogether too 'merry-eyed', imported a pretty 18 year old 'niece' to take over Nell's pleasantest domestic duties, she fed them regally - on poisoned pie. For her pains she was buried alive. And at night you can still hear her screams in the Dark Entry.

The 'Jackdaw', a recidevist like all his kind, atole the glittering ring of the Lord Cardinal Archbishop of Rheims and was cursed resoundingly and comprehensively:

> *'He cursed him in waking, he cursed him in sleeping;*
> *He cursed him in coughing, in sneezing, in winking . . .'*

But, to his eternal credit, just as comprehensively absolved him when the ring was found. And the jackdaw once again 'hopped about with a gait devout'.

In the 'Smuggler's Leap', Exciseman Gill on his 'high-stepping' mare, and rascally Smuggler Bill both died when sea-mist suddenly swirled about the Acol chalk pit: 'Makes one's flesh creep . . . where it yawns full 60 feet deep'.

In 1845, Barham was stunned by the death of a much loved son; caught a chill at the Queen's opening of the Royal Exchange; neglected it; had his uvula cruelly coated with caustic by two bone-headed doctors. Yet still joked gamely as, for the last time, he passed Amen Corner, to die, only shortly after his restless pen had scrawled:

> *'As I lay a-thynkynge, a-thynkynge, the golden sun was sinking;*
> *O merrie sang that Birde as it glittered on her breast.*
> *As I lay a-thynkynge, her meaning was exprest,*
> *"Follow, follow me away;*
> *It boots not to delay."*
> *Twas so she seemed to say,*
> *"Here is Rest".*

Quotation:
'An unrivalled humorist, a poet, a genealogist, an antiquary, a clergyman greatly beloved'.
Epitaph on a plaque on 61 Burgate, Canterbury.

6

BATES, Herbert Ernest (1905-1974)
Master of Diversity . . .

'HERBERT ERNEST' is hardly the stuff of which great novelists are made. Not surprisingly, to his friends . . . his wife . . . and even his children he was always the friendlier, rather more upper crust H.E.

Such names sprang from a family proud of its untarnished respectability; and of its never having been so much as a farthing in debt. His mother had started 'twisting threads' when she was just 10. His father was a shoemaker, constantly moithered by new-fangled machinery but with a great passion for the countryside which in long walks he passed on to his son.

Mediocrity however dogged H.E.'s early footsteps: a frail School Certificate could do no more than lead him to a job tying up endless parcels with endless brown cord. For all that the seed was germinating. When he was only 21, 'The Two Sisters', still undaunted after nine rejections, made its way to publisher Jonathan Cape. Their reader, Edward Garnett, later H.E.'s mentor, hailed a new genius - a Miss Bates!

Initially, short stories were his forte. 'I never had the slightest interest in long-winded plots. They were stories set among the countryside and with rural characters; stories superficially slow-moving but written with perception and vitality. Compelling dialogue too: never a word too many, never a word too few. Portraits were suggested by a few telling strokes rather than tired and overworked detail. Among them leery, gooseberry-crunching Uncle Silas 'of epic individuality' was unforgettable: 'a sinister little crab-apple of a man, a wencher, a liar, a poacher, a toper . . . with a lust for cowslip wine'.

Still young, H.E. and his much loved wife, Madge, left the flatlands of Northamptonshire to explore the hills and lanes of Kent. And at Little Chart Forstal they found 'The Granary'. It desperately needed repair and demanded a worthier setting. H.E. gave it both: with the help of an old Cornishman, a young Marsh lad, and jobbing gardener, Mr Pimpkin: 'En arf bin some weather, en it?'

Precariously balanced on the swaying tightrope of insolvency, H.E. wrote far into the night, 'Until my hand trembled and words danced before my eyes. My work was my life'. 'The Granary' looked onto open countryside. Today, H.E.'s gift to the village, it is the loveliest of village cricket grounds with its own wickedly tempting pond. Gradually the garden became an oasis of great beauty: 'the still centre of the turning world'. H.E. 'wrote as lovingly as he gardened; gardened as lovingly as he wrote'. His 'Love of Flowers' is proof of that.

His books and novellas received critical recognition. They had 'All the tenderness and delicacy of a Renoir landscape'; could intermingle comedy and tragedy; and paint evocative scenes. But it took World War II to help him catch a wider public; to stiffen their sinews for the dark years ahead.

Appointed a Flight Lieutenant in the R.A.F. Public Relations Section he lived with those ordinary, extraordinary 'Few', learnt their fears and hopes; immortalised them in short stories such as 'The Greatest People in the World' and 'How Sleep the Brave' under the pseudonym of Flying Officer X. Despite author anonymity, a war-sated public were inspired to buy some 2,000,000 copies. And then to seek other books from the same rivetting pen. At last royalties flooded in.

That pen and a growing maturity flowed into 'Fair Stood the Wind for France' (1944): a love story amid the terror and cold-blooded bravery of the Resistance. And on into 'The Purple Plain' (1947) and 'The Jacaranda Tree' (1949). Both were set in Burma. The former was a tale of the quiet gallantry, and the refusal-to-be-beaten of a pilot carrying his badly injured observer through Jap held territory to safety.

And after 'Love for Lydia' (1952) came a six-year lapse . . . until, seeking forgotten Easter eggs in a Kent village shop, he came face to face with Pop and with Ma Larkin in the all too generous flesh. Renoir sensitivity was sacrificed to Reubens lushness. 'The Darling Buds of May' was born. Pop and Ma Larkin ('two yards wide'), drunk with the fullness of life, blasted their way ostentatiously through the peace of the Kentish countryside with their six children, virtually damned at birth with overblown names: Mariette, Montgomery, Petunia, Zinnia . . . Rabelaisian and earthy, 'pungent as kippers and whisky', they showed a new side of H.E., one that T.V., film and the reading public loved. 'Perfick'. Not as far as I'm concerned, however.

Then, in 1969, like a butterfly from its ugly chrysalis, emerged 'The World in Ripeness', beautifully illustrated by the Kent R.A., John Ward. Two other equally delightful biographies followed.

The last was completed not long before H.E. died in Kent & Canterbury Hospital: on the edge of the City and in sight of Kentish grass and trees at the St Lawrence Cricket Ground.

Quotation:
'His best stories impress not so much by their strength as by their fragility'.
David Garnett (son of Edward Garnett)

BEHN, Aphra (1640-1689)

The Mata Hari of Restoration England . . .

IN biographical dictionaries, Behn follows hot on the heels of that pillar of domesticity, Mrs Beeton (Kentish too). But there is little in Aphra's life of domesticity. From poverty and imprisonment she clawed her way to the top, against fierce competition, as a playwright. She was the first woman to earn her living professionally by writing, when it was considered 'much too immodest and forward' for a lady.

Little of her early life can be gleaned even from 'The Life and Memoirs of Aphra Behn' by 'A Member of the Fair Sex'. It is a moot point as to whether she was born at Harbledown near Canterbury of a yeoman farmer, or at Wye, near Ashford, of the village barber, or even in Sturry, of . . .

What *is* known is that in 1663 she sailed to the West Indies with her family. Sailed to Surinam, still a virtual wilderness, where her father, barber or farmer, had been appointed to act as Governor. But it was a position to which he never succeeded as he died en route and was buried at sea.

Consequently Aphra's stay was short but long enough to inspire, in later years, her exotic but grim and moving novel named 'Oronooko'. In it she showed that even the slaves there, the Noble Savages, stood head and shoulders above their cruel and hypocritical owners. Oronooko himself, a prince among slaves, could 'run and wrestle better; chase snakes and tigers'. Her book was another first as no other writer until then had ever shown such open sympathy for slaves.

In 1666, a momentous year, she returned penniless to find London unrecognisable, cruelly ravaged by the Great Fire. And in a few months she was wed to a rich City merchant; widowed by a festering Plague; and enlisted by Charles II to act as 'She-spy' in Antwerp where danger threatened. Her beauty doubtless helped to wheedle Dutch plans of attack from renegade Englishmen high and foolish on schnapps. Transmitted back to England under her code-name Astrea they could, should, have spared England the ignominy of de Ruyter's devastating sweep up the Medway. But Charles' ears were as deaf to her warnings as to her pleas for money enough to cover her bare expenses. Clothes, and even her rings, had had to be pawned.

On her return from Holland she 'cryed herself dead' but still the Merry Monarch was deaf to all except his expensive mistresses. Imprisonment followed. And after despair came anger and a fierce determination. Her experiences became the catalyst for her nineteen plays, thirteen novels and three volumes of poetry.

Forced thus to write for her very bread she shrewdly studied the market: there comedy and bawdiness romped side by side in the rip-roaring, anything-goes era of the Restoration. She struck the same high note but with odious hypocrisy, her fellow writers denounced her plays as 'Lewd and unseemly coming from a woman's pen'; and Aphra herself as 'a reproach to womanhood'. It was a charge that critic Ernest Baker was to stir up some 200 years later: 'False, lurid and depraved' he trumpeted in words surely more applicable to a modern tabloid. But to Virginia Woolf, Aphra had 'courage, vitality and humour'.

Aphra rose boldly to the challenge with biting countercharges. Was she not following men's lead in bawdiness? Was it not remarkable that the women to whom they denied education could write at all? Surely bawdiness was not solely man's prerogative.

Her sharp-edged tongue was allied to a swiftly kindled temper. Probably never more so than when, before the curtain rose on her second play, 'The Dutch Lover', 'A wretched, ill-favoured fop, an officer in masquerade, opened what passed for his mouth' and in shrill falsetto announced to the audience at large, 'T'will be woeful. T'is by a woman'. He was 'A sorry animal that had naught to shield it from the uttermost contempt of all mankind but that respect we offer to rats and toads'.

Her pen was biting as well as bawdy. Two centuries ahead of her time she urged Women's Lib. In novel and play alike, particularly in 'The Forced Marriage', she missed no chance of swingeing attack on ill-matched unions: marriages for lucre and land, rather than for love; innocent young women of good family being married off to simpering fops with 'expectations', or to wealthy old rakes.

Aphra's last years were plagued by arthritis, by injuries sustained when her coach had overturned on an icy road . . . and by V.D. It was all that her lover, John Hoyle, a worthless lawyer, had given her before he moved on to his next conquest. In her blind obsession Aphra had written to him 'I grow desperate fond of you. I can have no thought of any other man'. But it had been to no avail. No matter: she still wrote five novels in her last eighteen months of life.

She was buried, in 1689, in Westminster Abbey. Not among her peers in Poets' Corner but in a shadowy cloister. Even this acknowledgement of her spirit and her skills was held to be 'a sad reflection' on Bishop Sprat who had dared allow burial of 'so lewd a woman' in Holy Ground. But Sir Peter Lely's portrait of the 'incomparable Astrea', highhanded, generous and indomitable, is in the National Portrait Gallery for all to see.

Quotation: *'Here lies proof that wit can never be*
A proof against mortality'.
Aphra Behn's epitaph.

BOLEYN, Anne (1504-1536)

Wife or Wanton . . . ?

THINK of Anne Boleyn as you will; as a bobby-soxer of her age, gazing in starry-eyed admiration at young Henry Percy, heir of the Earl of Northumberland, and his 500 richly liveried retainers; as a witty teenager flirting with handsome Sir Thomas Wyatt, poet, courtier and knight, 'thunderstruck' by her vivacity; as a tempestuous woman fighting with the ferocity of a tigress to achieve and to retain her proud title, Queen of England; as a woman, sadly wronged and condemned by her King who had sworn eternal love, yet, facing death, pleading for the lives of her fellow accused.

But have you ever thought of her as skilled with the pen?

To her father

Sir, I understand by your letter that you wish that I shall be of all virtuous repute when I come to the Court and you inform me that the Queen (Queen Claude of France) will take the trouble to converse with me, which rejoices me greatly to think of talking with a person so wise and virtuous. This will make me have greater desire to continue to speak French well and also spell, especially because you have so recommended me to do, and with my own hand I inform you that I will observe it the best I can. Sir, I beg you to excuse me if my letter is badly written . . .

Your very humble and obedient daughter
Anna de Boullan

Written from Kent's Hever Castle, her childhood home and later the scene of Henry VIII's courting.

* * * * *

To Cardinal Wolsey

My Lord, the which (his health) I pray God long to continue as I am most bound to pray - for I do know the great pains and trouble that you have taken for me, both day and night, is never likely to be recompensed on my part but only in loving you, next to the King's Grace, above all creatures living.

To Henry VIII

Sir, How great soever may be the bounties I have received, the joy I feel by being loved by a King whom I adore, and to whom I would with pleasure make a sacrifice of my heart if fortune had rendered it worthy of being offered to him, will ever be infinitely greater.

A letter to Henry VIII on her Court appointment as Maid of Honour - to the Queen she was to supplant.

Sir, Your Grace's displeasure and my imprisonment are things so strange unto me, as what to write, or what to excuse, I am altogether ignorant . . .
. . . My last and only request shall be that only myself shall bear the burthen of Your Grace's displeasure and that it may not touch the innocent souls of those poor gentlemen who, as I understand, are likewise in strait imprisonment for my sake. If ever I have found favour in your sight, if ever the name of Anne Boleyn hath been pleasing to your ears, then let me obtain this request and I will so leave to trouble Your Grace any further, with mine earnest prayers to the Trinity to have Your Grace in His good keeping and to direct you in all your actions. From my doleful prison in the Tower this sixth of May,
    Your most loyal and ever faithful wife
    Anne Boleyn

Her last letter before execution to the man who had sworn undying love.

> **Quotation:**
> *'For something like five years she succeeded in holding Henry VIII at arms' length, a remarkable performance . . . probably indicative that there was considerably more of cold calculation than of passion in her attitude'.*
> *Conyers Read in 'The Tudors'*

BROOKE, Jocelyn (1908-1966)
Orchid hunter . . .

YOUNGEST son of a Folkestone man who had rejected Law for Wine. The latter he then sold with the same dignified and decorous solemnity with which he had previously dispensed legal advice. Jocelyn remembered him as 'gray, charming and rather disconsolate'.

For young Brooke, flowers were more attractive than people. As a result, even at the tender age of four, he could identify plants shown on the colour plates of Edward Step's 'Wayside and Woodland Blossoms'. And 'precocious little beast that I was, I learnt their Latin names too'. At six, in his own words, he was 'a polymorphous pervert'. He had a not unnatural love for his nurse, a rather less natural one for a friend of similar age; and, distinctly strange, fellow feelings for Pompey, a Pomeranian, in particular . . . and polecats in general.

He lived then on Sandgate's respectable Undercliff in pine-scented air and within sound of the sea pounding on shingle. But he longed to pass the toll-bar at its end for the forbidden fruit of the funfair, whelk stalls, and milling crowds of trippers. Old enough, he went to King's School in Canterbury, didn't like it and - ran away! Was promptly returned; and as promptly ran away again. Finally he found Bedale's kindlier co-educational ethos more to his liking than the macho one of King's. This, despite a nearly demented mistress, driven to despair by his unmusical ear, storming at him. 'I will not, I simply . . . will . . . not . . . continue to teach music to a moron'.

To three years at Worcester College, Oxford, he added three years in a bookshop before reluctantly joining the family business. 'Trade' did not suit him, so he courteously resigned. And, instead, found solace in solitary walks in the Elham Valley, and on the Downs above it where, with perseverance, orchids could be found. Orchids in general, 'Yes'; the rare Military Orchid, 'No'. The search to find it actually growing became as imperative as the Arthurian knights' quest for the Holy Grail.

Zealously though he sought it there and on the Downs at Wye and Crundale, it eluded him. Eventually he was forced to recognise that 'like scarlet and pipe-clayed uniforms, like Housman's Lancers and Ouida's Guardsmen, and the whole conception of War as a chivalrous and honourable calling, it had vanished, to be seen no more.

His own experience of war came in 1939. He immediately volunteered for the R.A.M.C; served with it in North Africa and Italy, tending the wounded, the shell shocked, and then (himself ostracized like a leper) those to whom V.D. was preferable to yet more front-line horror. In 1945, to the astonishment and derision of his rejoicing fellows, he signed on again in the Regular Army. But peace-time soldiering was not war-time soldiering. So, with the slender royalties from 'The Military Orchid', he bought himself out when a cystolic heart murmur and possible promotion to sergeant threatened his comparatively tranquil life as a Corporal.

Writing and botanizing became his life. 'The Botanical History of the English Wild Orchid' was his magnus opus. His 'Orchid Trilogy' consisting of 'Military Orchid', 'Mine of Serpents' and 'The Goose Cathedral' were unusual hybrids, part fiction, part autobiography, seamlessly joined. A mixture of reminiscence and reflection, they had all a hybrid's unusual beauty. The former dealt mainly with his quest for that rarest of orchids. The second vividly displayed his love for the forgotten, vast and demonic art of pyrotechnics as well as the fire-works of night life in Paris and London. And the latter painted a fascinating picture of the pseudo-Gothic 'cathedral' of the Folkestone Lifeboat Station - with, of course, its grotesque gaggle of geese.

Brooke willingly admitted that he was literarily lazy and his work too formless. But there lies much of its rare charm. His featherlight pen wafts the reader, effortlessly as a Magic Carpet, from Taormina and Palermo to the East Kent villages of Lower Hardres and Acrise; from Bedale's classrooms to Field Dressing Stations from elegant and formidable Aunt Cock to Ninnie, his childhood nurse. Painless transitions in clear, spare prose where nature and human nature are seen through a poet's eyes.

His books never sold as they deserved and today, rare as his orchids, they are sought more for a steadily growing investment value than for their own intrinsic worth. He had therefore to use his literary talents in other directions: BBC Talks producer; leader writer for the 'Spectator'; and oddly, in the Elham Valley, literary critic for the 'New York Herald Tribune'!

Though for a time he had enjoyed the liberating discipline of a private in the R.A.M.C. he grew to hate conformity; the noise and bustle and ugliness of modern town life. From it he retreated to the peaceful haven of Bishopsbourne. It lies in the valley of the erratic Nailbourne, legendarily decreed by an irate Devil to flow only once in seven years, and below the Downs. It would have been hard to find a more tranquil place.

There too, perhaps, he communed with that other quiet man of letters, the priest and theologian, Richard Hooker of whose words in 'Ecclesiastical Polity', the Pope wrote ' . . . they shall last until the fire shall consume all learning'. And with Joseph Conrad, teller of tales of the sea, who had lived at Oswalds, hard by Hooker's old rectory. They lay not a hundred yards from Brooke's own house, Ivy Cottage: tiny, crouching in the shadow of a much taller neighbour but with three proud dormer windows in its tiled roof, and sturdy chimney-stacks.

Today, it is festooned with roses and bears a simple ceramic plaque; one decorated of course with ivy and orchids. It was the kindly thought of a neighbour who felt that, despite all his glowing memories, Brooke had, in the last years of his life there, been a sad and lonely man.

Quotation:
'Here is a new writer of very fine quality'.
Lord David Cecil

BURNETT, Frances (Eliza) Hodgson (1849-1924)

The Barbara Cartland of her Day . . .

THOUGH she spent much of her life in America, her two most famous books, 'Little Lord Fauntleroy' and 'The Secret Garden', are English to the core. And a not inconsiderable amount of her writing was done in Kent at Great Maytham Hall, Rolvenden.

She died wealthy but she was born into comparative poverty - in Cheetham Hill, Manchester. Even there, the enthusiastic young gardener-to-be found that 'The back garden is always full of wonders - a Garden of Eden'. And when her father's failing ironmongery business fell on even harder times, because of the American Civil War, and forced them to move to a less pleasant district, she wrote sadly of ' . . . slightly soiled daisies and buttercups in the local park'.

When her father died, her mother fought gamely on until, in 1865, they swapped ironmongery for groceries - with an uncle who lived in Knoxville, Tennessee! There the romantic stories she had loved to tell at home were scribbled down in white heat onto paper - six pot-boilers a month! Within a year, although Frances was only 17, Sarah Josepha Hale (who had given a grateful world 'Mary Had a Little Lamb') was discerning enough to see solid talent beneath the lush coatings of sickly sentimentality. And so did Scribner's! Frances was well on her way to wealth.

In 1877, marriage - after seven years courtship - and her first, and best novel, 'That Lass O' Lowrie's' (a realistic Lancashire saga later turned into a successful play) went hand in hand. Swan Moses Burnett was an ear, nose and throat specialist but when success came knocking ever more frequently at Frances' door, he found time to be her enthusiastic and capable agent. The only snag was that, as he became ever more interested in her books . . . he became ever less interested in her. With that, an ever-widening life style, and her own breakneck pace of writing, they slowly drifted into divorce. Besides that, she had from the very first hated that stupid Christian name – Swan!

Sadly, it was out of the fire . . . and into the arms of a ne'er do well medical student-cum-aspiring actor. Here surely there was a heady mixture of Romance? But within three years that marriage also had foundered.

Good however came out of ill. For, celebrating her second marriage, she had, in 1898, in one of her ever more frequent Trans-Atlantic journeys back to England, leased Great Maytham Hall. It stands just outside Rolvenden, with its spacious High Street flanked by tile-hung and white weather-boarded cottages, and on a ridge between the differing beauties of Weald and Marsh. Now here again was Romance!

In 1893 it had been ravaged by fire and as carelessly botched up with mock Tudor timbers and Gothic gables. The fact that it had 18 bedrooms, a smoking room, a billiard room . . . stables and piggeries . . . and a long-neglected orchard in no way deterred her.

It had been built, in 1721, by a Captain Monypenny, R.N. out of hard won prize money from the capture of a French man o' war. Unfortunately, it had to wait 40 years for the solace of a roof until his son, a future JP, had, by the gentlemanly pastimes of smuggling and gambling re-established the Monypenny fortune. A proof of the latter slightly scurrilous assumption is the 400 yard underground tunnel from the Hall's vaulted cellars to a shadowy copse.

Until the lease terminated in 1907, Frances flung herself enthusiastically into village life as the Grande Dame - but it was the huge, walled garden which held her enchanted. Roses were planted prodigally to clamber over the gnarled and twisted trunks of the apple trees ('In the Garden', however, was published only posthumously, in 1935). And there she found the ideal 'study' in which to write, with a nearby gazebo as a handy wet or windy weather retreat. Admidst this idyllic scene some 14 of her books were written.

And the neighbours? Hardly a stone's throw away was Hole Park full of memories of Edward Gibbon of 'Decline and Fall' fame. Only a little further away was half-timbered Smallhythe Place - and Ellen Terry, England's greatest Shakespearean actress of her day (who wrote ceaseless loving letters to the Irish literary iconoclast, G.B.S.). At Burwash there was Rudyard Kipling; and at Rye, fellow Anglo-American Henry James who recognised her ability to spin stories for children but, as a famed and fastidious pillar of literature, discreetly distanced himself from his flamboyant neighbour.

Had Frances known it, still more romance lay ahead for Great Maytham Hall. In 1910 it was virtually re-built by Sir Edwin Landseer Lutyens, designer of the London Cenotaph; bought by Thomas Cook of travel fame; requisitioned by the Army; turned film star in 'Dunkirk' because of its resemblance to a French chateau; slowly decayed; and after its chance discovery by a horrified Tunbridge Wells landscape architect, given a much needed face lift; and settled down to happy semi-retirement as apartments for the well-to-do.

Her two best known books, however, were not among the 14 she wrote at Great Maytham Hall. 'Little Lord Fauntleroy' was written before she had even settled there - but running to some 30 editions it was to make her fortune. Its young American-born Earl-to-be was based on her Parisian-born son, Vivian, whose life it was said 'was thereby ruined'. The too-good-to-be-true seven year old with flowing golden locks, lace collar, black velvet suit, light blue cummerbund, silk stockings and buckled shoes, who was based on him, was the bane of a long life. Doubtless too that of hundreds of other boys thrust into similar clothes by proud mammas, heedless of the taunts of friend and foe alike.

The last years of her life were spent in America in a hazy dream world of mystical religions - which did nothing to prevent her tyannising her own family. Let's hope it was there that 'Fluffy' gained her over-blown, candy-floss appearance, her love of frilly clothing, and an obsession for wigs which surely could owe nothing to rural Rolvenden. Manchester and Kent perhaps may share a little of the blame for the self-centred, gushing schoolgirl that lay beneath the veneer of an author who wrote over 70 books and plays, 20 of them for children.

At the time, her books, derided today, were raptuously welcomed despite - perhaps because of - her sentimentality and excessive romanticism. Reviewing her last book, 'Robin', the Times Literary Supplement said it all, succinctly, in the single word 'Syrup!'

> **Quotation:**
> *'The most satisfying children's books I know'.*
> *Surprisingly - Marghanita Laski*

CHAUCER, Geoffrey (c. 1340-1400)

Poetry's Pageant Master . . .

ENGLAND'S first great poet! But, born in London, a vintner's son, he is neither Man of Kent nor Kentish Man. Nevertheless, imperiously, he demands inclusion. Didn't the King himself appoint him Justice of the Peace for Kent; and a Knight of the Shire who represented that county in Parliament? Wasn't he a King's Messenger and Nuncio who frequently travelled the whole width of Kent from London to Dover on royal business?

Besides who else has travelled it so entertainingly? Travelled it from Southwark's Tabard Inn, amid brothels and breweries, leper hospitals and lime-kilns, to the bed-bugs, fleas and three-in-a-bed of Canterbury's pilgrims' hostel, The Chequers of the Hope. But first, of course, to the very purpose of their pilgrimage, to the jewel-studded shrine of Thomas à Becket, 'that holy, blissful martyr'.

At 12, as page to the Countess of Ulster, he early learnt true courtesy. Some use of arms too; for in due course, he was sent on an expedition - a military fiasco, at Ratters in 1360. There he was captured and held to ransom - until Edward III thought highly enough of him to pay the £16 demanded for his release - a rather less sum than that he immediately paid to release Sir Robert de Clinton's charger!

From his journeys to France and Italy he brought the sweet music of rhyme, some of the courtly love of 'Roman de la Rose', and the smoothly phrased tales of aristocratic passion in Bocaccio's Decameron. He could write too with economical delicacy:

> *'Now with his love; now in the cold grave, alone*
> *Withouten any company'.*

His work ranged from the highly moral to, as Melvyn Bragg neatly puts it, the 'wincingly bawdy' all in the racy idiom of his day.

Things looked up when he joined John o' Gaunt's household. There he wrote 'The Book of the Duchess', a tender elegy on the death of the latter's wife. But in 1386, shattered by loss of patron, pension and wife within a year, he sought solace in 'The Canterbury Tales'. He had already published 'Treatise on the Astrolabe', 'written for little Lewis, my son, in English for Latin he cannot yet read'.

In his master work, his themes are as pertinent today as they were 600 years ago. And his pageant of characters is equally unforgettable. The 'gap-toothed and red-stockinged, tightly-gartered' Wife of Bath (surely an Agony Aunt of her day?) who, when asked what women longed for most, bluntly replied, 'Wommen desiren have soveryntee'. After all:

> 'She'd had five husbands, all at the church door,
> Apart from other company in her youth;
> No need to speak of that forsooth'.

Logic was not her strong suit for in almost the same breath she would assert that virginity was 'great perfection' . . . and celibacy, 'contemptible'.

The red-bearded, black-nostrilled battering ram of a Miller, tells a tale of cuckoldry so bawdy that Chaucer advises his more genteel readers to skip it,

> 'Wrangler and buffoon, he had a store
> Of tavern stories, filthy in the main'.

Contrastingly, the honey-tongued Pardoner preached vehemently against gambling and avarice - but he was a charlatan and racketeer . . .

> 'For in his trunk he had a pillow case
> Which he asserted was Our Lady's Veil'.

There were others too of course, equally ear-catching. The coy Nun, 'all sentiment and tender heart'; the Friar, 'a wanton one and merry'; the Cook, 'stood alone for boiling chickens with a marrow bone'; the Skipper, 'the nicer rules of conscience he ignored'; and the Parson, 'hated cursing to extort a fee'. A marvellous medieval cross-section from the Knight 'ever honoured for his noble graces' to the Summoner 'who drank till all was hazy'. As Dryden said, 'Here is God's plenty'.

James Lowell recommended that anyone doubting Chaucer's 20th century readability should first undertake a 'penitential course' of Chaucer's contemporary, John Gower, who 'raised tediousness to the precision of a science'. Even cold figures support Chaucer's warm reputation, for 'The Canterbury Tales' has sold more copies than any other book except the Bible. And for 600 years he has surely done great service for Kent as 'Publicity Agent', unpaid.

Quotation:
'I take unceasing delight in Chaucer'.
Samuel Taylor Coleridge

CHURCHILL, Sir Winston Leonard Spencer (1874-1965)

Leader of an Embattled Nation . . .

EVERY reader knows his record as a man of action. He fought with Sir Bindon Blood against Pathans on the North-West Frontier; charged the Mahdi's power-drunk Dervishes at Omdurman (1898); infuriated Army Authorities as a hybrid subaltern-cum-war correspondent at Spion Kop; escaped Boer capture after being ambushed near Durban - with a derisory £25 price tag on his head; and after being made the scapegoat in 1915 for the Dardanelles disaster, served at the front for two years in World War I as a Lieutenant Colonel.

In 1900 the man of action became the man of the spoken word. In the House of Commons he was held to be the greatest orator since Charles James Fox. There, over the years, he offered the nation he was to lead to victory 'only, blood, sweat and tears'. There too, with England virtually defenceless, he defied German might: 'We shall fight on the beaches, on the landing grounds, we shall fight in the fields and in the streets, we shall fight in the hills, we shall never surrender!'.

It was there too that he paid fitting tribute to the indomitable Battle of Britain pilots: 'Never in the field of human conflict was so much owed by so many to so few'. He even jested with the French: 'Nous attendons l'invasion promise de longue date. Les poissons aussi'. His sonorous words, and his unshakeable confidence, inspired the nation. But, he maintained, it was the *people* who had the lion heart - he had merely supplied the roar.

As a man of letters, his books have never had the same popularity but they are nevertheless remarkable literary achievements. His wide reading of Gibbon and Macaulay (later Trollope and the Brontes) became 'the anvil on which he forged an intensely idiosyncratic style'. During the thirties, when out of office, he found solace in writing the epic story of his blood relation, England's 18th century military saviour, the Duke of Marlborough. He started too on his four-volume 'History of the English Speaking Nations' - finished after the War despite his having had a minor stroke. After the War too came his major achievement, the six-volume 'History of World War II'. And in 1953 he was awarded the Nobel Prize for Literature. More gripping for the layman but now long out of print, were the 1,000 page 'River War', 'London to Ladysmith via Pretoria' and 'Thoughts and Adventures'.

Much of his life was spent in Kent; much of his writing done at his home, Chartwell, near Westerham. For him the Study was its heart. There he wrote as 'stimulus and intoxication' with a wide-ranging mind and a sense of history. Wrote too out of financial necessity for he had poured money into Chartwell to make it a unique house and garden. '2,000 words and 200 bricks a day' was his maxim. He laid bricks as accurately and effectively as he laid words - and had a Union card to prove it.

Churchill worked methodically and to a routine: a hearty English breakfast in bed at 8.30; 'Times' and 'Telegraph' scanned; then, still comfortably in bed at a set temperature of 74⁻F, he wrote - and dictated even as he dressed for lunch. After it he relaxed in the garden, feeding his black swans and Canada geese, strolling with his unpopular, malodorous sheep, or communing with his long-lived golden orfe.

A cat-nap. Work. A cigar and a drink: 'Always remember I have taken more out of alcohol than alcohol has taken out of me'. And at midnight not to bed but again to the study with his 100 horse-power mind and his seven league boot imagination still pulsing . . . there to write until 3 or 4 in the morning. An 18-hour day!

The study itself was an inspiration. Its windows looked out onto the glory of beech-clad Crockham Hill, and across his own garden to the lakes he had helped to create. His wide mahogany work-table carried family photos; the walls, pictures of his aloof father and vivacious American mother, of war leaders Roosevelt and Stalin, of Blenheim Palace where he had been born prematurely. Eager to be in the thick of things?

There were busts too of the great men, Napoleon and Nelson, with whom he was to rank. And above all, from the open beams and rafters, hung the three standards he most cherished: Lord Warden of the Cinque Ports, Knight of the Garter, and a Union Jack, the first to be raised over a city freed from German tyranny, Rome.

Few man have ever created so much with - WORDS!

Quotations:
'In War - Resolution. In Defeat - Defiance.
In Victory - Magnaminity. In Peace - Goodwill'.

'There is no finer investment for any community than putting milk into babies'.
Winston Churchill

COWARD, Sir Noel Pierce (1899-1973)

Jack - and Master - of all theatrical skills . . .

'**I**AM an enormously talented man; after all, there's no use pretending that I'm not'. So, in all truth, wrote Noel Coward: pianist and dancer, lyricist and librettist, cabaret star and director, novelist and playwright.

This very remarkable man was born quite humbly: the son of a piano-tuner and a mother, who, though of 'Good Family', was to be reduced to taking in lodgers. Formal education played little part in his life; the stage, virtually everything. At six he brought down the house before an audience of doting mothers with a saccharine rendering of 'Coo' from 'The Country Girl'. To his own accompaniment, too!

A year or two later he won 1st prize on Bognor Regis beach from Uncle George and His Merrie Men's Concert Party. And there, having failed to produce a tragedy of his own imagining with the help of three reluctant little girls, he smote one on the head with his wooden spade. It was a unique breach of his own later dictum: 'Never - ever - lose your temper on the stage'.

At ten he made his first professional appearance, at 1½ guineas a week, as Prince Mussel in 'The Goldfish'. Other appearances followed: as Slightly in 'Peter Pan', Charley in 'Charley's Aunt', and at the Coliseum as understudy in 'A Little Fowl Play'. His only failure, to secure a place in the Chapel Royal Choir, astounded his ambitious mother as she had understood that Dr Alcock, the Royal Organist, had excellent connections both with the Royal Family and The Almighty - and should, therefore, have known better.

Despite these minor successes (and the élan of falling in love with a vivacious, ringletted 14 year old with a deliciously turned up nose who furthered his hitherto limited knowledge of sex with risqué stories*), family finances were at low ebb, and his beloved mother on the verge of a breakdown. To prevent this, from a Dymchurch house lent by actress Athene Seyler, he scoured Romney Marsh to find a peaceful cottage for her. Found it (at 10/- a week) strategically sited between the Star Inn and the church, at St Mary-in-the-Marsh. In the latter's graveyard, with a mossy tombstone at his back, he wrote much of 'The Queen was in her Counting House', incongruously situated in Ruritania. It was while staying here that he developed his deep love for the Marsh: 'Its lazy rivers, silvery green flatlands, huge skies and ever changing clouds'. But not the sunsets; they were: 'Too red, too affected'.

It was from St Mary's that he visited a boyhood heroine, Edith Nesbit (qv). As a child he had read each of her stories avidly as they were serialised in 'The Strand'. He had even stolen - and pawned - a necklace

---

* The inimitable Gertie Lawrence with whom he was to act frequently in the West End.

to get the 4/6d needed to buy 'The Magic City'. Each year, bewitched by their humour and easy flow, he re-read them all.

And it was from St Mary's too that he and his mother, from Aldington Knoll, caught a first glimpse of the farm that was to become their much loved home for 30 years: a square lopsided building with a staid Victorian air; jammed up against another building 'much perkier, with pink corrugated roof'.

When the seedy 'Vortex' made Noel's name and his fortune, they viewed it more closely. Found it 'poky, quite hideous - and with an outside loo!'. But at £500 and with a 'Room With a View' (and what a view!) . . . money and taste turned tumbledown farmhouse into smart country mansion. Certainly not a nouveau riche upstart 'which ate peas off its knife'.

Somerset Maugham's short-time wife Siri did her costly best with the decor. Folkestone, Deal and Dover, even Hurstmonceux Castle, were ransacked for antiques, Grinling Gibbons carvings were hunted down and carried home triumphantly. And so were *two* grand pianos.

It became a 'palace' fit for a theatrical king . . . for his mother . . . and father . . . and Auntie Vida. Former and latter fought bitterly and continuously with barbed tongues. It was only when Vida died that her sister mellowed: 'Doesn't she look pretty? What a pity she was so disagreeable when she was alive!'. His mother also enjoyed driving - driving as befitted a lady of Good Family. She ditched the vicar and his wife when they were out walking; and she precipitated herself and car through the plate-glass window into Peark's pyramids of tins.

The London West End theatre, from impresario Binkie Beaumont to the divine Gertrude Lawrence, swept down at weekends on 'Goldenhurst'. It took a war and an Army requisition to tear Noel from it for ten unduly long years. But he returned triumphant - on his 50th birthday. 'It was always a welcoming house'. And much of his best work was written there in the tranquility of the Marsh.

Coward was an outstanding craftsman; 'The Master' of satiric humour and shrewd and witty dialogue; of haunting melodies and bitter-sweet lyrics. His dramatic battle honours were unique.

Over 25 plays, ten musicals, seven films (in many of which he himself acted), four novels, a ballet, letters, diaries, hundreds of songs, and fascinating three-part 'Autobiography'. Of them, light comedy 'Home Chat' and Italian festa based 'Sirocco' were booed off the stage with catcalls, animal noises and even gross sucking imitations of kisses during the tenderest passages between Ivor Novello and Bunny Doble. 'Vortex', 'that dustbin of a play', dealing directly with drug addiction and obliquely with homosexuality, was rapturously given a long run.

Noel offered an exceptionally varied menu. 'Blithe Spirit', with Madame Arcati, an overpoweringly enthusiastic medium, who raised trouble as well as a still intransigent deceased wife, helped Laughter outface Fear throughout the War. In the operetta 'Bitter Sweet' (1929) old time melody and romance confronted modern Jazz. 'Private Lives', one of several comedies of manners, or of unmanners, dealt with an upper class couple who, neither able to live with, nor without, the other, meet again on their second honeymoons. 'This Happy Breed', (1943) with contrastingly plebeian but patriotic middle class comedy. And his engagingly named 'Nude with a Violin' (1954) was a satire on modern *art*.

On the screen, on a grey railway platform at Carnforth, there bloomed 'Brief Encounter': an illicit romance foredoomed to failure. In 'In Which We Serve' (1942) playboy Coward turned Mountbattenesque naval commander. And re-fought HMS Kelly's battle against the odds with German destroyers off Crete.

For sheer lavishness and lump-in-the-throat patriotism 'Cavalcade' (1931) was a runaway winner. It needed Drury Lane; a revolving stage with six lifts; 400 hungry extras; 3,500 dresses; and 30 years of proud imperial history, from the relief of Mafeking to World War I Armistice night. All was threaded through with nostalgic songs 'Soldiers of the Queen', 'Dolly Grey', 'Tipperary' . . .

At the outset of World War II Noel had hoped for a propaganda job in Paris - but Paris fell all too soon. Instead, Churchill ordered him: 'Go out and sing 'Mad Dogs and Englishmen' while the guns are firing - that's your job'. (Doubtless also, 'Don't put your daughter on the stage, Mrs Worthington').

In World War I, just beginning to climb the slippery theatrical ladder, he had pulled every possible string to avoid active service. In World War II he sought it. He toured huge camps, grim tented hospitals, even solitary gun sites . . . to boost troop morale.

In Australia tough Diggers came to harrass the effete Pommie with his clipped accent and stilted mannerisms. But under his spell they stayed to cheer him - and to chair him in triumph. With Bill Slim's forgotten Fourteenth Army in Burma he sang in the heat and humidity of the jungle only a thousand yards from the Japanese lines with the stench of rotting corpses in his nostrils. Sang before an exhausted audience snatched, for one forgetful hour, from the front line - and with their rifles ready across their knees.

In 1956, monstrous taxes drove him to Las Vegas and to Café de Paris cabaret . . . to America . . . and to a home in Jamaica. In 1970, it was left to a Labour government to fittingly recognise his services to stage and screen with a knighthood. And for the BBC to offer delighted viewers a glorious pot-pourri of Coward for a whole week!

Three years later, after murmuring 'See you tomorrow' he died in his sleep. An open book lay on his bedside table: Edith Nesbit's 'The Enchanted Castle'. A last reminder of Romney Marsh.

Quotation:
'Work is more fun than fun'.
Noel Coward

DICKENS, Charles (1812-1870)

'A National Possession' . . .

NO other novelist has ever created such a wide ranging army of unforgettable characters as those who march through the pages of his books: henpecked blacksmith Joe Gargery; oh, so humble Uriah Heep; dissolute but selfless Sydney Carton; slatternly drudge, the Marchionness - who found married bliss. And king of them all, jovial, accident-prone Mr Pickwick. No other author has been able to create such atmosphere; of London squalor, or pathos, of the death of Little Nell.

It was his irresponsible father, John Dickens, a clerk in the Naval Pay Office, who gave him the raw material for Mr Micawber: 'Talent Mr Micawber has; money Mr Micawber has not'. This was to be 'the damnable shadow' that haunted him, that drove him into the Marshalsea Prison.

But before that it was he, 'though not a great one for locomotion', who gave Charles his happiest memories of Kent. Of the mysterious Marshes; of brown-sailed barges on the Thames; of Gad's Hill Place which even at 10 he wanted for his own but sighed, 'Though that's impossible, Father'; of Rochester's alleys, castle and cathedral; of a review, on Chatham Lines, of the 43rd and 52nd Light Infantry; and of the grim convict hulks lying off the Dockyard. All found a place in his books.

So when, in 1821, redundancy forced Mr Dickens to London, it was with a very heavy heart that Charles left Kent behind him as he rode 'packed like game; carriage paid' in The Commodore which he long remembered, 'smelling of damp straw'. London was to be a horrendous change. With the last stick of furniture pawned, the whole family, except for Charles, joined Mr Dickens in the Marshalsea. With a remarkable £6 a week coming in and with the services of a young maid (Marchionness-to-be) they fared far better than Charles did in his seedy Camden Town lodgings.

From them he had to walk, early and late, four miles to the dilapidated Hungerford Stairs warehouse, alive with scurrying rats, where he worked. Worked from morning till night labelling bottles of Warren's Blacking, alongside a dozen 'common men and boys'. Worked, moreover, in the window before which louts and layabouts stopped to grin and jeer. For a sensitive 12 year old, it was indeed 'Such an agony of soul'.

But something, a legacy, did turn up for 'Mr Micawber'. Penitent and ashamed, he sent Charles back to school. This, despite the protests of Mrs Dickens, of which her heartbroken son was to write, 'I *shall* never forget; I *can* never forget'. Charles' Heaven from Hell was the 'Classical and Commercial Academy'. Its Head was a Welshman; not surprisingly, a Mr Jones. A man 'who could never resist beating a plump boy' and who drilled his pupils far less effectively than they drilled their white mice during his lessons.

On such a slender education, Charles nevertheless found work briefly in a solicitor's office. And to escape it wrestled with the 'despotic characters' of shorthand so successfully that by 18 he was the 'Morning Chronicle's' star of the Press Gallery. It was a job that on occasions took him to report meetings in a distant town. And, headed for home, to scribble shorthand notes on the palm of his hand by the light of a dark lantern in a wildly galloping postchaise and four as they raced for London - to be first with the news.

Spreading his wings, he was also beginning to have cameo articles, such as 'Dinner at Poplar Walk', accepted. Even to have, in 1836, new, go-ahead publishers Chapman & Hall actually publish his first book 'Sketches by Boz' which included much meatier 'Bedlam', 'The Drunkard's Death' and 'Visit to Newgate'. Why Boz? From his adenoidal young brother Augustus Moses, who could manage no more for his name than 'Boses'.

And from 'Boz' he raced on to 'Pickwick' - and marriage - by sheer chance. Established illustrator Robert Seymour had dreamt up a series of ludicrous mishaps to a Club of ludicrous sportsmen. Needing a literary collaborator he wrote offering the job to one Thomas Clarke, (author of 'Three Courses and a Dessert'). For reasons never known he did not reply. It was Charles's chance; he seized it with both hands. And with the help of brilliant Cruikshank illustrations - for the unhappy Seymour had just committed suicide. Pickwick was well enough reviewed but rather sluggish in sales until Sam Weller made his invigorating bow. Then, monthly sales of 4,000 rocketted to 40,000! And in three years Charles had netted a very considerable $10,000 thanks also to 'Oliver Twist' and 'Nicholas Nickleby'.

Now, financially secure, he could consider marriage. When only a 19 year old nobody he had ardently courted Maria Beadnell, a wealthy banker's pretty daughter. He 'adored her, every minute, day and night' but she played him disdainfully, like a fish. Then 'with heartless indifference, cruelty and coldness' left him to founder out of his depth. But for all that he never forgot her!

On the rebound, his attention turned to a publisher's daughter, Catharine Hogarth. Plump and placid, 'Kate' had heavily lidded blue eyes but little else to offer. Restive, even before the last days of their honeymoon (in 1837, at Chalk, near Rochester) love-blinded Charles must have sensed that 'uninterested and uninteresting' she would always be hopelessly outgunned by his own dynamic personality.

So it was. In fifteen years she bore him nine lively children and suffered four miscarriages. In moments of noisy depression he tended to consider that the children were solely of her doing. All were named, rather oddly, after writers: Alfred D'Orsay Tennyson Dickens; Kate Macready Dickens; Edward Bulwer-Lytton Dickens! With Charles often too busy and 'Kate' hopelessly incapable, their upbringing was largely in the hands of Georgy, Aunt Georgina (Kate's sister).

They drifted steadily apart, until, in 1858, they agreed to separate. Perhaps it was the advent of Number Ten: 'a compliment I could well have dispensed with' that decided the issue. A very relieved Dickens made her 'as generous a settlement as if she had been a lady of distinction and I a man of great wealth'.

He also hastened to publish a letter subtly hinting that separation was more Kate's wish than his. And that contrary to 'most grossly false, most monstrous, most cruel accusations,' no breath of scandal must attach to the 18 year old actress, Ellen Ternan. 'There is not in this earth' he wrote, surely overdoing it, 'a more virtuous and spotless creature'. And yet, she was to be quietly tucked away as his rather reluctant mistress for twelve years.

The discomforts of travel never deterred Dickens. He frequently stayed abroad and he also bought a travelling-carriage, one so heavy that 6 or 7 mph was its top speed, and passengers had not infrequently to walk uphill. In this way they journeyed through France to Valence, Avignon and Marseilles, there to relax on a steamer bound for Genoa which they found was 'a city in decay'. Piacenza's ramparts were ruinous and grass-grown. In Parma, Corregio's frescoes were mouldering; even Rome was unimpressive. But Pisa, their base, was unforgettably lovely. And Venice - Venice was The Magnificent!

His first journey to America, to write a travel book, had been a very different matter. It was a triumphal progress rather than a mere tourist jaunt. A tour however that might never have been, for howling storms lashed the Britannia's paddle-boxes to matchwood, hurled lifeboats overboard . . . And, as a ludicrous finale, the Captain ignominiously stranded them on a mud-bank in front of Halifax's expectant crowds.

In America he addressed both Houses; was cheered and fêted wherever he went, be it by canal boat, stage coach or steam boat. Only two clouds, no, three, marred those exciting days: America's unashamed piracy of his books with their blank refusal to accept copyright. Slavery that horrified the radical in him. And fierce criticism of his criticism. Later, his rather derogatory Martin Chuzzlewit was to be publicly burnt in New York.

Dickens was glad to be home. Broadstairs might not be Baltimore or Buffalo but it was 'a place which they enjoyed amazingly'. From Bleak House, high above the harbour, he would bound down to its quay - to yarn with the old salts; to organise quadrilles to the music of his comb; to clamber down onto its 'rare good sands' and walk until he was 'salmon-coloured as a porpoise'; and to dance at the Tivoli Gardens.

Every Eden has its snake. The transistors of their age, 'an inferno of excruciating organs, fiddles, bells, glee singers . . '. drove Dickens to the peace of - Boulogne and its Ramparts.

In 1856, the now wealthy author bought Gad's Hill Place, the mansion which he had coveted as a penniless boy. There he worked in the wooden chalet given him by the actor Fechter; held weekend parties; romped with his dogs which were granted free access to the bowling green by hog-holes in the surrounding hedge; mourned 'Dick, the best of birds' and took long walks through the Kentish countryside.

Books continued to stream from his pen; 'Little Dorrit', 'Bleak House', 'The Tale of Two Cities' . . . Then, in 1858, his love of the pen was side-tracked by his love of the stage. Acting each part, he gave readings of his most famous passages; put them across so dramatically that he was as one with an audience that wept or laughed uncontrollably under his hypnotic spell. And after each he was drained physically and emotionally: 'I am become incapable of rest'.

In between his four tours, one utterly exhausting to America, he was involved in a railway disaster near Staplehurst. Every carriage of the up Tidal Express plunged into the River Beult - except his. Although himself in shock, Dickens worked tirelessly among the dead (11), the dying, and the injured (40). Despite this, he pleaded with his doctors for one last tour - a tour which virtually killed him.

In 1870, in very poor health, he was at Gad's Hill writing the 24th chapter of 'The Mystery of Edwin Drood', set in Rochester, when he had a seizure. And died. He had always wished to be buried near Gad's Hill with its view 'over the pensive Cobham Woods'. Rochester Cathedral offered him a resting place but was refused. Westminster Abbey, for so great a man, demanded the honour - and got it. It was there, with no funereally plumed horses; with 'no black cloaks, bows, long hatbands or other such revolting absurdities', England's greatest novelist was privately laid to rest. For two days, thousands filed past his open grave. 'No other Englishman' said Bagehot, 'had attained such a hold on so vast a populace'.

Quotation:
'As a young champion of the disinherited, he fought for humanity and justice'.

DURRELL, Lawrence George (1912-1990)

Poet, Pianist and Pied Piper of Lovers . . .

HE was born almost as far away from Kent as it is possible to be - in the foothills of the Himalayas, near Darjeeling. But, like others in this book, he gains admission because, when he was only 12 it was Canterbury he came to for his education.

Unlike Maugham and Walpole, Pater and Marlowe, he did not go to King's School. The credit, such as it is, is St Edmund's, a Church school perched high above the City on the way to Whitstable. But it must be sadly admitted that neither saint nor City were to improve his later sexual mores.

Perhaps 'credit' is used mistakenly for, without modesty or shame, he once admitted 'Intellectually I am brilliant - but like all Irishmen I was dreadfully lazy'. And because of that Achilles heel he repeatedly failed the qualifying examination for Oxbridge that he could so easily have passed. He stuck at it though because 'above all, my subconscious was intent on proving to my father that it was unfair to send me back to a prison'. So much for sadly maligned St Edmund's!

Liberated eventually, he headed joyously for London hot-spots. There he worked as a jazz pianist at the Blue Peter Night Club. Soon after, as estate agent and odd job man. Then, with his better known zoologist brother, Gerald of 'Bafut Beagles' fame, he persuaded his widowed mother to move lock, stock and barrel from staid Bournemouth to the sunnier and less conventional climes of Corfu, that 'idyllic island with a blood-stained history'.

He was driven to writing, he said, by his sheer ineptitude in other jobs. Inept too perhaps in writing, for his first novel 'Pied Piper of Lovers' (1935) was an abysmal failure with only a handful of copies sold. For his second book 'Panic Spring' he took refuge behind the pseudonym of Charles Norden.

It was with 'Bitter Lemons', however, that he made his reputation by evocatively capturing the spirit, the very essence of Corfu, as he was to do with other Mediterranean islands, in lush 'purple patches' as ripe as their fruit. Landscape, he maintained, dictates our behaviour and even thought. The interlocking 'Alexandria Quartet' was 'an investigation into love', set amid the exotic and Bohemian life of that cosmopolitan city where he had worked as Press Officer during the war.

Versatile, he also wrote critiques, plays, travel books and 'White Eagles Over Serbia', a rousing book for boys; 'The Black Book', even more rousing, was a book for adults - so much so in fact that no reputable English publisher would touch it.

'Antrobus Complete', with its tales of diplomatic life, was Wodehouseian rather than Rabelaisian; whilst' Caesar's Vast Ghost' hauntingly described his second love, Provence. To his sternest critics he was however 'a semi-erudite populariser', one whose verse ranged bewilderingly 'from the fastidious to the vulgar'. To others, 'a novelist of originality, and poet of some quality'.

Perhaps it was his 'investigation into love' that sparked off his four marriages. And perhaps it was his Irish conceit, 'I have always had such a good physique and such intense charm that it is difficult to be true to oneself', that brought three of them to disastrous ends. No matter which, in this feat he was outdone by his long-time friend and co-editor of the Paris-born magazine 'The Booster': Henry Miller of 'Tropic of Cancer' ill-fame, who initially backed up his slender literary earnings by living on those of a Broadway taxi-dancer!

It was at Sommieres, in Provence, that he died after a long struggle with emphysema.

Quotation:
'If you really worship women they will forgive you anything'.
L. G. Durrell

'DISGUSTED' of TUNBRIDGE WELLS
Swingeing scribes . . .

Anonymous and vitriolic gentlemen who, at the turn of the century, erupted regularly in 'The Times' in Letters to the Editor. Probably an indignation (to coin a new collective noun) of disgruntled majors, ex-Indian Army, retired, who, returning to the Old Country found 'Gad, Sir, it's gone to the dogs!'. And trumpeted to that effect at every innovative modern trend. Their name became a by-word for deep-dyed, darkest blue Toryism.

Quotation:
'He'd have been horse-whipped in my time!'
'Disgusted'

FERMOR, Patrick Leigh (1915-)

'A wandering writer, he . . .'

IN 1918 Fermor was 'orphaned' - when, hardly weaned, and his mother and older sister set sail for India to join his father, the Director of Geological Survey - he was left behind 'until the seas were safer'!

Patrick too was shipped off - much less romantically - to deepest Northamptonshire for four supremely happy years with a kindly farming family. There, 'discipline' was almost a dirty word, and a smack as rare as lambing in July.

On his mother's return four years later Patrick fought belligerently shy of this demanding stranger. Visits to 'Peter Pan', record-breaking 'Chu Chin Chow', and 'Where the Rainbow Ends' lured him back into the family fold. Even so, kindergarten, his sister's girls' school, and 'a truly horrible Prep School' all ended in unconstrained disaster.

In desperation two psychiatrists were called in. (One of them had treated authoress Virginia Woolf before she filled her pockets with stones and walked into the River Ouse). Salsham Hall - a contemporary of A. S. Neill's 'Do as you like' Summerhill School - was recommended. It was run by a wild-eyed Major Truthful (honestly!) and a staff heavy with bangles and beads.

Its pupils included an epileptic musical genius; an Admiral's kleptomaniac daughter; a pursuivant's son who suffered nightmares; and a millionnaire's son who belaboured passing cars. On wet afternoons, all, stark naked, danced through 'Gathering Peacods', 'Selligers Round' and 'Old Mole' in the barn to the accompaniament of a reedy recorder. Patrick loved it all. 'Fay ce que vouldras' was indeed his motto.

When such unconstrained days ended he went on to pass Common Entrance at a rural crammers, relaxed also but refined. Ahead loomed King's School, Canterbury, 'a school of improbable antiquity'. Patrick did not view life there with the same trepidation experienced by authors-to-be Hugh Walpole and Somerset Maugham, and classical scholar Walter Pater, all of whom were subjected to bullying.

Contrastingly, Patrick loved its medieval buildings, monastic brewhouse and bakery, surrounding the spacious Green Court; the line of towering elms; the towers and pinnacles of the Cathedral seen mistily through them; infirmary ruins and the Dark Entry beneath the Lattergate (where the Rev Richard Barham in rhyming jest, as ever, interred Nell Cook alive for serving her priestly employer and his new mistress with a poisoned pie).

King's School itself, with its strict rules and traditions, its energetic monitorial canings, and a record breaking impositional mileage of Latin hexameters, was just a challenge; a chance to show off. To do, in today's moronic catchphrase, 'Anything for a laugh'. He was out of bounds nearly as often as he was in them - at night too.

This, with a slowly gathering sex drive, led him to his downfall. Long before Page Three, long-necked, wide-eyed, Pre-Raphaelite girls who variously became ice-maidens, water-sprites and goose-girls had ensnared him heart and soul.

So now did a local greengrocer's daughter, 24 year old Nellie. Stunned perhaps by his ceaseless bombardment of sonnets she allowed a decorous holding of hands - no more. Unfortunately King's distinctive straw boaters and winged collars made him as conspicuous as a felon in broad arrows. Authority tracked him down. And, with no small relief, demanded his departure.

What then? Backed by a remarkably charitable letter of recommendation from his long-suffering Housemaster, he ironically made a serious attempt to enter the discipline of Sandhurst. Again, it all came to nothing: soldiering suddenly lost its glamour; an urge to write bubbled within him; and he shared a flat in Shepherd's Market, then a residential retreat rather than today's raffish red light district. Instead, Life with neighbouring Bright Young Things took precedence.

In the midst of it - a sudden, irresistible urge! Kitted out from Millett's Army Surplus Stores he set off on a bleak winter's night to walk - from the Hook of Holland to Constantinople! A four year, 3000 mile Odyssey. He wrote as he walked. But the story was published evocatively and with Anglo-Irish flair, only in 1977, 'A Time of Gifts'. The second instalment, 'Budapest to the Iron Gates', was not published until 1986.

It was a journey that took him from Cologne and Heidelberg to Stuttgart and Salzburg, from Prague and Vienna to Budapest and Constantinople. Took him along the Rhine and the Danube, across the Carpathians and the Alps, and through Transylvanian forests. Wherever he went he made both short-term and enduring friendships; experienced much kindness and hospitality; and saw some of the burgeoning horrors of rampant Nazism.

Adventure and wanderlust took over again in 1942. Then, dashingly black-turbaned, be-sashed and cloaked, and with silver and ivory dagger in his belt he fought in the mountains alongside the Albanian, Cretan and Greek guerillas against the Nazi invaders. This was no play-acting for he captured, and smuggled back to England, the German Commander, General Kriepe himself!

Quotation:
'On these Augsburg choir stalls, highly polished, free-standing scenes of Biblical bloodshed ran riot'.
Patrick Fermor

FLEMING, Ian Lancaster (1908-1964)

Labour Leader Hugh Gaitskell's Favourite Fantasist . . .

BEING born into wealth (his grandfather, Robert Fleming had been a very prosperous merchant banker) gave Fleming a flying start when, much later, it came to describing 007's high life style.

First, not surprisingly, he graced Eton where he was Victor Ludorum for two years. On, briefly, to Sandhurst and then - not the Army - but private education in Munich and Geneva. In 1929, there followed a job - with Reuters - in Moscow! Life in that drab city must have palled for in 1933 he returned to his roots as banker and stockbroker.

It took World War II to bring glamour back into his new career as the handsome, uniformed P.A. to the Director of Naval Intelligence. In that position he travelled widely. One of his ideas, far more fantastic than any Bond incident which he later dreamt up, was to confront Rudolph Hess (described by Churchill as 'the maggot in the German apple' when he secretly flew into Scotland to plead for Anglo-German detente) with Aleister Crowley, disciple of the occult and self-styled 'wickedest man alive'.

Fleming celebrated the end of the war in style by building his cherished home, 'Golden Eye' on the Jamaican coast. There his near-neighbour was Noel Coward who thought even less of Fleming's cuisine than of his slapdash literary style.

Women fell in droves for his handsome, Hollywood star good looks. Perhaps even for his offhand approach. To his diary he confided, 'Older women are best as they think it may well be for the last time'. In general, he wanted women 'he could turn on and off like a light switch'. It was novelist Rosamond Lehmann who put her finger squarely on it: 'He gets off with women simply because he can't get on with them'.

For all that, his appointment as Foreign Manager for the 'Sunday Times' gave him the opportunity, at 44, at last to marry his longtime love, Ann Charteris. And, in addition, to emerge from the decade-old shadow of his brother Peter whose 'Brazilian Adventure' had been a 30's best-seller. Another brother had been one of the élite 'Death or Glory' squads to be left 'underground' in Kent to act as saboteurs behind the German lines should their invasion succeed.

From such a background, James Bond 'Licensed to Kill' was born in 1954 in 'Casino Royale'. It was written, rather desperately, and in only a few weeks, 'to take his mind off his imminent marriage'. From such a quick conception 007 was to thrive lustily in a further 11 novels and 7 short stories: saving the world (with the help and, on occasion, the hindrance of a succession of luscious girls) from the clutches of ruthless megalomaniacs who made Genghiz Khan look like an immature schoolboy. In them, it was said, he 'technologised the fairy tale'. Writing in the early days was largely for fun; in later ones, for finance. Despite his rocketting success he had no pretensions: 'My books are straight pillow fantasies of the bang-bang, kiss-kiss variety'.

To a vast following of readers he added an even vaster one of cinema buffs. For delightfully named film director Albert R. Broccoli gave Bond on the screen even more girls and even more of the gadgetry that became his hallmark than he had ever had on paper. There was no shadow of doubt that even the comparatively discreet 'Sex, Sadism and Snobbery' of the post-war years paid him handsome dividends.

In England, Ian Fleming lived rather less exotically - but almost equally beautifully - than he had in Jamaica. His house stood at the very foot of Dover's White Cliffs, and on the very edge of the English Channel at St Margaret's Bay. (Again Noel Coward was his neighbour). The ancient Cinque Port of Sandwich, and his Mecca, the world famous Royal St George's Golf Course, were little more than a three-iron shot away. For him, it was 'the best golf course in the whole world'. It was there (only thinly disguised as St Mark's to avoid offence to its élite all male membership) that 007 played a much deadlier game with Goldfinger.

Fleming loved 'the early morning song of the lark . . . the rich fragrance of wild garlic . . . the rigour of the game in general . . . and the prestige of 'George's' in particular. So when, in 1964, he was proposed for the high office of Captain of the Royal St George's Golf Club it was a peak even in his high-powered life.

But Fate, as in so many of his novels, took a hand. Only two days before the ceremony, Ian Fleming suffered a severe haemhorrage . . . was rushed by ambulance 15 miles across country to the Kent and Canterbury Hospital . . . and died there. Died with his last ambition unfulfilled.

James Bond had killed again. This time his victim was of real flesh and blood. For it was overwork on 40 million Bond books, in 10 years; that had been the root cause of his death.

Not that Bond died with Fleming . . . Within the year Kingsley Amis, author of 'Lucky Jim' and 'Quizzical Drinking', had written not only 'The James Bond Dossier' but also, under the pseudonym of Robert Markham, had had the effrontery to write 'Colonel Sun' - with James Bond, secret agent, as its central character.

Fleming's wife, Ann dismissed it scornfully as 'petit bourgeois, red-brick Bond'. Today, the original, vintage 007 lives on in nationwide popularity of films and books alike.

Quotation:
'I regard "Goldfinger" as an obscene book, liable to corrupt'.
Harold Nicolson
(Hardly in a position to throw bricks?)

GOSSON, Stephen (1554-1624)

Theatrical turncoat . . .

GOSSON, playwright and pamphleteer, was descended from butchers on his mother's side, and carpenters on his father's. Like the infinitely more famous Christopher Marlowe he was Canterbury born, St George's Church baptized, and, as a day boy, King's School educated before going to Corpus Christi at Oxford. Thereafter, as he himself more pessimistically put it: 'Pulled from my university before I was ripe - I withered in the country for lack of sap'.

For all that he made his mark - and his way to London. There he first became noted 'for his admirable penning of pastorals'; and was ranked, perhaps only by his closest friends, with Edmund Spenser of 'Faerie Queen' fame. Despite that he turned player; and a little later, writer of plays and tragedies as bawdy and violent as those in which he had acted.

In 1579 came a *volte face* as swift and fierce as a skulking tiger's return to its kill. His 'Schools of Abuse', as slashing an attack as any in literature, ranted against the theatre in florid euphemism. It was, he wrote, 'a pleasaunt invective against Poets, Pipers, Players, Jesters and suchlike Caterpillars of a Commonwealth'. 'Pleasaunt' was hardly the word for it!

Well in his stride, he then rounded on the theatres themselves: 'Such a Gordian knot of disorder in every playhouse'. A keen blade indeed was needed to cut through it. They were 'markets of bawdry where every paramour and his wanton first met, and where there were straunge consortes of melody to tickle the ears'. (The Pop music of his age?)

Harmless recreation such as playing cards and bowling alleys also felt the prick of his sharp wit. A final wild thrust dispatched even more harmless University dons 'who coope themselves up fortie yeres together studying all things - and finally professing nothing'.

This diatribe was dedicated to a singularly unappreciative 'Maister' Philip Sidney of Penshurst Place. That gallant intellectual was unimpressed. Gosson received neither patronage nor shekels but only scorn for his pains. Good, however, came from evil. For Sidney was fired to write his famous 'Defence of Poetry'.

Gosson's onslaught did not go unanswered. Playwright Thomas Lodge (who later warned youthful spendthrifts to mend their ways in 'Alarum against Usurers') counter-attacked in 1580 with 'Defence of Players' - and added scurrilous personal comments for good measure. The 'Plaiers' themselves had only recently, in 1572, been equated by Parliament with 'Rogues and vagabonds and sturdie beggars' all of whom were liable for whipping, and ear-piercing with a one-inch red-hot iron. Fearlessly they hit back. Tongue in cheek they staged two of Gosson's own bawdy plays; and a morality of their own 'To hold up all theatre ill-wishers to contempt and ridicule'.

From Gosson's vitriolic pen there also came 'Pleasaunt Quippes for Upstart Gentlewomen'. It was a coarse satire and bitter tirade aimed at women's 'monstrous abuse' in the extravagant apparel they affected. A less acidic, even helpful, 'Short Treatise of Lawful and Unlawful Recreation' also came from his pen.

In 1584, acrobatic *volte face* again! In London, pamphleteer turned priest. First lecturer at Stepney Church, with a handsome stipend of £30 p.a.; and then to St Botolph's in Bishopsgate. It was, however, from St Paul's Cross, the Speakers' Corner of his day, that he trenchantly upheld the war against Spain in 'The Trumpet of Warre'. And it was at Bishopsgate that the fearless Gosson was 'buried in the nighte'.

Quotation:
'Is it not strange in this our vain age
To see one climbe to Pulpit from the Stage?'
Linsie Wolsie

GOSTLING, William (1696-1777)

Ailing antiquarian . . .

STAMPED through and through with 'Canterbury' - as indelibly as a piece of Margate rock - for Gostling, the Cathedral loomed large in his life. He was baptized there, married there, and, like his father, John, was Minor Canon there - for 50 years. Was educated in its very shadow at King's School. And was remembered there, together with all his large family (four of whom under three years died in the space of two sad years), on a marble plaque. Years later it fell and was shattered on the Cloisters' paving. William lived in - and loved - Canterbury virtually all his life.

His father, in his old age, had a genius for snapping up vicarless benefices; in his youth, was a member of the Chapel Royal Choir singing with outstanding power, tone and compass. It was a fine voice that William inherited. An intrigued Charles II, having been told that eggs were good for a singer's voice, generously gave him one - of silver, filled with gold coins.

Yet he was nearly the cause of John's death. Once he took him aboard the new royal yacht, 'Fubbs' (named after his mistress, the Lady Castlemaine) to 'provide sweet music'. A howling gale, far from musical, would have swept them disastrously onto the Thanet cliffs had not the King himself hauled on the ropes as desperately as his panic-stricken crew.

William's one excursion to 'foreign parts' was no further than Cambridge whence he returned with B.A. and M.A., as swiftly as coach and horses could carry him to Canterbury. He loved and knew its every history-steeped stone and brick; and delighted in guiding complete strangers and tourists (especially Americans still loyal to England) round its walls.

Not unnaturally he wrote a book (in 1774), entitled 'A Walk in and About the City of Canterbury'. As lighthearted as its author, it was far and away the best book since William Somner's 'The Antiquities of Canterbury' (which, all unwittingly, had acted as 'card and compass' in guiding the Puritan iconoclast Blue Dick to hidden glass, sculpture and paintings for his gleeful destruction).

Gostling was a modest man but one who knew his own worth - and was not afraid to say so. 'With many observations not published elsewhere' he boasted on its title page. And later, added, 'I had no scruple to differ with other writers'. His book was a treasure house of architectural detail - much of which he hadn't seen for some years.

For a decade he had been confined to bed or chair in his house in the Mint Yard in The Precincts. Age and gout had been 'great hindrances'; except as a trencherman, for he could still demolish a haunch of venison at a sitting. Yet 'sometimes I was not able to hold a pen for weeks or months'. But, he maintained, 'my memory was still pretty good'. And when it did occasionally falter his daughter and his friends became his eyes and legs.

It was for her, without house or money after his death, that a second edition was printed. She had looked after his home full of working models, and gadgets such as the perspective glass that he had developed to save craning his neck as he looked 130 feet up at Bell Harry Tower's superb vaulting. And she had had to usher in a ceaseless flow of visitors (said, one year, to exceed 2,000, including the King of Poland).

The list of subscribers for this edition ranged from the Dowager Countess of Aylesford to the Most Reverend Archbishop of York. En route it took in the Archbishop of Canterbury, a Countess, a couple of Dukes and Duchesses, a quartet of Earls, and much of the Army from Cornet Tipping of the Dragoons to Lt General Williamson of the Artillery. And the fact that the Prebendary of Westminster helped round off the list by buying *two* copies was surely final testimony of its worth.

Undoubtedly his 'Walks' was his magnus opus. For the rest, he wrote of natural wonders: 'The Sinking of Some Land at Lympne' in 1727, and 'An Account of a Fireball and Explosion in Canterbury' in 1741. But it was in a biographical curiosity that he showed his versatility by turning the prose 'Peregrinations' of his friend Hogarth into lively verse. The young artist and four roistering companions, all well in their cups, suddenly decided upon a tour of Kent.

'From Covent Garden we took departure
To see the world by land and water.
Our march did with a song begin,

36

Our hearts were light, our breeches thin.
We meet of nothing of adventure
Till Billingsgate's Dark House we enter
Where we diverted were while baiting
With ribaldry not worth relating
(Quite suited to that dirty place!)'.

One night, at the 'Nagg's Head', at Nether Stowe (where no nightcaps were provided!) they not only slept in sheets oozing damp but they 'awakened at three and Cursed our Day for Eyes, Lips, Hands being tormented and swollen by the Biting of Gnats'. A setback but they roistered happily on with adolescent pranks, high good humour and frequent libations of 'good Flip'.

'Though by the way we did not fail
To stop and take three pots of ale
And this enabled us by ten
At Rochester to drink again'.

It was such an adolescent saga that antiquarian Gostling turned into several pages of rollicking, if execrable, verse.

Quotation:
'My limbs though they are lame, I find,
Have put no fetters on my mind'.
William Gostling

HARDWICK, Michael and Mollie (Michael 1924-1991)

Typewriter Duet . . .

PROBABLY the most remarkable husband and wife writing team in the world. If only the MCC had an opening pair who scored runs as consistently and regularly as they wrote books! And as fast scoring too - for 150,000 words in a fortnight were a mere bagatelle to them.

As script editors and producers they had worked alongside at the BBC until they decided to remain permanently alongside in a marriage that never faltered. Yorkist and Lancastrian

37

though they were born, it was rarely a Battle of the Roses. Working for the BBC necessitated a London home: an 18th century, book-crammed house in Highgate Village. Here, Hudson and Bellamy, as individual as their celebrated TV namesakes, held feline sway.

Then, with London too claustrophobic, they headed (during the 1962 Great Freeze) for much- and long-loved Kent; for Great Mongeham, near Deal; for Ivy House, a 17th century Brewmaster's home. There they met Margate-born Alfred Deller, the internationally famous counter-tenor who was discovered by Michael Tippett when he was a Canterbury Cathedral choirboy. And it was in Deller's superb 15th century half-timbered house, near Ashford, that they spent much of their later life.

Mollie's first book, recording a royal visit to New Zealand in 1954, was written in an astounding two weeks. As she wrote one of her bestsellers, 'The Duchess of Duke Street', dispatch riders waited outside to rush each chapter as it came from the typewriter to her London publishers. Every year she turned out at least one historical romance: 'Beauty's Daughter' won the 1976 Elizabeth Goudge Award of the Romantic Novelists' Association. Romantic too, and percipient as well, were her biographies: 'Emma, Lady Hamilton'; 'Mrs Dizzy', part fact, part fiction; and 'Private Life of Sherlock Holmes', wholly imaginary!

Michael was even more versatile. No false modesty about him! He dared complete the 'Mystery of Edwin Drood' for Charles Dickens; write a Sherlock Holmes novel, 'Prisoner of the Devil', as good as any from Conan Doyle's pen; and, as a challenge to himself, and 'for the good of his soul', he dreamt up a sequence of 'Regency' books: 'Royal', 'Rake', 'Revenge', 'Revels' . . . But then he was reputed to be descended from Queen Victoria's father, George III's fourth son!

As a sideline he abridged all Trollope's Palliser novels. And, still more a *tour de force*, he reduced Barchester Chronicles' million words to 150,000 yet kept Trollope's style and spirit alive. This to a fortnight's deadline for a BBC television series - and much of it done in hospital!

Add to that a biography of Alfred Deller, 'A Singularity of Voice'; A 'Charles Dickens Companion'; Guides to Oscar Wilde, Sherlock Holmes and G.B.S.; 'Literary Atlas and Gazeteer'; and 'Writers' Houses' (many in Kent). All have become unmatchable reference books. And as pot-boilers he also wrote 'The Discovery of Japan' and 'The Plague and Fire of London'.

In collaboration with his wife there were still more books. Books of TV films: 'Bergerac', 'Tenko' . . . while 'Upstairs, Downstairs' alone spawned nine books, including 'Mr Hudson's Diary'. Hundreds of play scripts;

magazine features; book and restaurant reviews for Kent Life and Kent Messenger . . .

Both Michael and Mollie could claim over a hundred books each. Many of them were composed straight onto typewriters in the same study where interruption of one by the other was permitted only 'by appointment'. And each could adopt the other's style . . . to write successive chapters in one book.

Before settling down to freelance journalism, Michael had worked in New Zealand. Been a reporter too. And to that attributed his almost uncanny knack of being on time for even the most demanding deadline. In his later years he and his wife somehow found time to be columnists for both 'Kent Messenger' and 'Kent Life'.

Michael's greatest acclaim was undoubtedly in America where his Sherlock Holmes titles 'Sherlock Holmes, My Life and Crimes' (an autobiography written in the first person); various novels; and, as a climax, 'The Complete Guide to Sherlock Holmes', were enormously popular. So popular indeed that his twelfth title alone sold 50,000 copies. On its publication he spent 4½ non-stop hours signing hundreds of them for a queue that had to be controlled by the police!

One Hardwick fan, thrilled to learn there was a 'Sherlock Crater' on the moon, spent four years lobbying for a mountain in Oklahoma to be named Holmes Peak. Michael was naturally invited to the ceremony, presented with Sheriff's star and stetson, and made an Honorary Marshal of Oklahoma!

During World War II he served in India and on cessation of hostilities was transferred to Tokyo - as officer i/c Tokyo Grand Central Station! On its platform he met (saluting was forbidden by Army decree) the former Son of Heaven, the Emperor Hirohito, seeking to show his people that he had democratically shaken off his legendary cloak of divinity and immortality.

Michael and Mollie Hardwick were a truly remarkable couple who must have given immense pleasure to literally, and literarily, millions.

Quotation:
'Elementary, my dear Hardwick'.
Christine King

HARMSWORTH, Alfred Charles William, Viscount Northcliffe (1865-1922)

From 'Comic Cuts' to 'The Times' ...

THE oldest of the thirteen children of an English barrister and his Irish wife. At first he seemed to be a rather lumpy, run-of-the-mill boy, one with no great ability or future . . . But that was only until he was 13 . . . Then, a great career was sparked off by a cheap and simple toy - a jelly-graph which reproduced in rich violet ink.

That was it! From editor of an amateur school magazine (encouraged by his headmaster, J. V. Milne, father of A. A. who, at 6, was already a valued contributor) he rocketted to Press baron, one who owned 3,000 square miles of forest in Newfoundland; thundering presses that turned out 5000 tons of newsprint each year; vast paper mills on the Thames; and imposing offices over the old Fleet river.

Fortunately, a shrewd business brain grew alongside jelly-graph productions. Intuitively he realised that there was a growing market, one born of the 1870 Education Act, that wanted reading matter, simple but lively and spicey. So, when a pharmaceutical chemist named Newnes published 'Titbits' (which is precisely what it was) he spurred Harmsworth into action.

In 1888 Alfred gave a clamorous public just what it wanted in 'Answers to Correspondents' which sold at one penny and contained articles such as 'Why Jews Don't Ride Bicycles'. Within a year he had boosted a very viable magazine into a sure-fire winner with a brainwave. He offered a 'Pound a Week for Life' to the reader who could most exactly estimate the value of gold and silver on that day in the Bank of England vaults. The winner guessed to within £2! It brought Harmsworth notoriety and 3,000,000 new readers.

Not forgetting the kids, 'Comic Cuts' (and 'Chips' solely to discourage competition) followed soon after. H. G. Wells, who had happily contributed to 'Titbits' was holier than thou later when he wrote, not a little pompously, 'It has a complete disregard for good taste, educational influence, or social consequences'. And his former headmaster wrote: 'Harmsworth killed the penny dreadful - by producing a ha'penny dreadfuller'.

But from there on Harmsworth climbed the ladder to success with giant steps . . . In 1894 he bought the 'Evening News'; in 1896 founded the 'Daily Mail'; and in 1908, after secret negotiations and reducing the price to 1d, stood on the topmost rung when he took control of 'The Times'. Talked about at 20 he was famous at 30 . . . and with a Viscountcy to boot in 1904. His title, Northcliffe, was taken from the little Kentish seaside town of Broadstairs, which sheltered sunnily under the North Foreland. And was where he had spent his honeymoon.

He chose his staff shrewdly and, it was said, paid his editors like Prime Ministers. But for all that, G. B. Shaw, by now famous as a dramatic critic, complained bitterly but unavailingly that his notices were often cut to the bone or even omitted altogether. 'I'm not running my paper just to please a damned Socialist' Harmsworth snarled. 'You look as if there were a famine in the land' Harmsworth once complained. 'And you as if you were the cause of it' swiftly returned the vegetarian.

A kinder side of his nature was shown with another famous contributor, Edgar Wallace, who could knock out a thriller in under a fortnight. But he overstepped himself when he advertised the 'Four Just Men' all over London on hoarding, tube and train. The basic circulation of 38,000 did zoom but expenses zoomed even faster. It was Northcliffe who saved him from bankruptcy.

Alfred was a vain man; a dull man some said. No word of criticism of him was ever printed in any of his papers. 'That's just plain bad psychology' growled his monkey-faced rival, Beaverbrook of the 'Express': 'Any publicity is good publicity.' But his open attack on Lord Kitchener did lose him 300,000 affronted readers.

Broadstairs had long been a favourite holiday haunt. In 1889, the good-natured horse that pulled his dog-cart and stopped now and then to admire the view, did just that - in front of 'Elmwood'. Over the garden wall he saw a modernised Tudor house set in a beautiful garden with its own pool. The very next day Harmsworth, shamelessly gazumping another eager buyer in the process, bought the house. Billiard room, hot-houses, stables for old-fashioned horses, garages for modern cars, soon followed. So did rich furnishings from Liberty's of London, and a telegraphic nerve centre from which he kept Fleet Street on its toes.

In its garden, among other things, he grew melons and peaches: kept prize pigs; and, separately of course, a pampered Florida alligator that wintered in the comparative warmth of the town's Clockhouse Conservatory. Amid such luxury, Hollywood's first famous stars, Mary Pickford, 'the world's sweetheart', and Douglas Fairbanks, the swash-buckling Thief of Bagdhad, had their honeymoon.

Paradise gained! And Paradise so nearly lost. In 1917, Northcliffe, on the recommendation of his near neighbour, John Buchan of '39 Steps' fame, had been made Director of Propaganda in Enemy Countries. It was a job he did so effectively that on 25th February, G85, a German destroyer, crept in under cover of darkness to shell the clearly silhouetted 'Elmwood'. Northcliffe, a fatalist, slept through the attack. But only 100 yards away, the gardener's cottage was hit. And Mrs Morgan and two of her six children died. Two months later they were avenged by HMS Broke of the Dover Patrol.

Dog-cart gave way to a fleet of cars. Northcliffe was nothing if not innovative. He was one of the first motorists and one who took part in the first London to Brighton run in 1896 which tore away the shackles of a 3 mph speed limit that had originally been designed for snorting steam traction-engines. He was also involved in the first recorded car accident in Kent. In swerving to avoid a horse, his chauffeur overturned the car - and Northcliffe was temporarily paralysed. He was a believer too in the new fangled flying machines and in wireless telegraphy.

The Napoleon of Fleet Street died comparatively young, 57, but he never lost his love of Broadstairs. Anonymously he did much-good work there - and through his generosity a succession of Poplar boys first knew the joys of a seaside holiday. Golfers too benefitted for it was he who drove off at the inauguration of his £50,000 North Foreland Golf Course.

'He was' his rival Lord Beaverbrook said, '. . . the greatest figure who ever strode down Fleet Street'.

> **Quotation:**
> *'Have you heard? The P.M. has resigned.*
> *Northcliffe has sent for the King'.*

HEATH, Sir Edward Richard George (1916-)

Paradoxical Premier; Best Selling Author . . .

THE little seaside town of Broadstairs, Dickens favourite watering place, runs a remarkable gamut of literary talent. Not a little incongruously, it ranges from Frank Richards, creator of Billy and Bessie Bunter, to - Edward Heath, Prime Minister of the United Kingdom.

On 9th July, 1916, he arrived there with a bang. For that same night German naval units shelled nearby Ramsgate. A loner, aloof, uncommunicative, often rude and unappreciative, he inherited little from his father, a genial extrovert carpenter who rose to become Builder and Decorator. Much however from his mother, a lady's maid, who had learnt the virtues of hard work, public responsibility and service, and had inculcated them into her son. Of morality too, for she forbade bathing with a cousin - young, but already over-generously endowed! Heath never married; he was already married to politics.

Even at St Peter's Primary he outstripped all the others in brain as well as bulk. And when, having won a scholarship to Chatham House Grammar School in Ramsgate, he finally left, it was with reports that were not so much reports as eulogies. Left too with his headmaster's words ringing in his ears: 'That boy could become Prime Minister'.

A flaw in this jewel? He did not succeed in passing the Scholarship Exam to his Nirvana, Balliol College, Oxford, until he was 19. And that with his English Literature result dismissed as 'Definitely worse' than that of his first attempt.

Despite that, his occasional articles were gladly accepted by 'Isis' (which later he threatened to sue when it dared to describe his father as a *jobbing builder!*). And when he was seeking adoption as Bexley's Parliamentary candidate, to cope with election expenses, he bolstered up a meagre Civil Service salary by acting as News Editor of the respected 'Church Times'. Writing certainly helped him to scramble up onto the first rung of that longest of ladders - as MP with a majority of 133 out of a total poll of 56,000! Not surprisingly perhaps he once told the Commons, 'The smell of printers' ink still makes my blood tingle'.

His distinguished political career has no place here - until it ended. Until, after only 3½ years as Premier, he ran aground on the jagged rocks of inflation and Union strikes. Well and truly beached, he was left glowering, sulking and out of office . . . but at least with unlimited time to indulge his three great loves: music, sailing and travel. More importantly, with time to write about them.

In 1975, he sat down and wrote a book on sailing that became a stunning best-seller. As a kid at Broadstairs it had been no more than messing about in dinghies. Later, as a 49 year old Leader of the Opposition, dinghies became a succession of ocean-going yachts: each a 'Morning Cloud'. The first was built at Upnor, on the Medway. No fairweather dilettante, he sailed, often in appalling weather, fiercely and competitively, with professional skill. He won the Admirals' Cup, the Round the Island race three times in succession, and, most prestigious of all, the Sydney to Hobart race.

Strangely, the carpenter's son had the sea in his blood and he sent it coursing through the 40,000 words of the lavishly illustrated 'Sailing: A Course of My Life'. Boosted by serialisation in the 'Sunday Times' it sold an astonishing 90,000 copies in its first year. Not bad going for a novice author?

Hard on its heels, in 1976, he wrote of a second love - music. When he was only ten his parents had yielded to his pleas and, for £42, bought him a Bobby Thornton piano they could ill afford. At 15 he was learning the still deeper pleasures of the organ. And also the art of conducting. It was one that he used joyously when for many years he conducted the Broadstairs Christmas Carol concerts in aid of the town's deprived children. Still more joyously doubtless when he conducted the Chinese Philharmonic, the Chicago Symphony Orchestra, and Andre Prévin's L.S.O in Cologne and Bonn, in Elgar's bravura piece 'Cockaigne'. It was in music that he expressed his political jubilation and frustration on his Steinway at No 10.

It all came pouring out in 'Music: A Joy for Life': his father's very words when he had given him that first piano.

'I love the freshness and spontaneity of Brahm's Third Symphony, the glorious exuberance of its opening, the simplicity of the slow movement, the sad lilt of the third, and the forceful jollity of the leaping tune of the last'.

Not quite such a rip-roaring success as 'Sailing' but it sold 42,000 copies in advance orders alone. A figure much boosted by a whirlwind publicity tour in a special train. During it he crammed in 11 television appearances, 37 broadcasts, numberless press interviews and whistle-stop signing sessions - 300 an hour at his best!

Placed third came 'People and Places'. With the former, on the whole he was not good but oddly he struck up lasting relationships with Mao Tse Tung and Deng Kiaoping so that visits to Peking were long an annual event - until Tianaman Square! As a schoolboy, a day trip to Paris had been his peak; as Premier, or roving Elder Statesman, in power or out, the world, except for Moscow and Eastern Europe, was his oyster. Heath delighted in travel - especially when it was his hosts who paid for his journey and for his steadily growing taste for luxury. Not quite as successful as 'Music' or 'Sailing' but he did take over 40,000 readers with him round the world on a fascinating tour.

And, as a pleasant and unusual runner-up, came 'Carols: The Joy of Christmas'. Braving bitter December winds howling across the North Foreland, he had, at 15, conducted 'Our Carol Party' to raise money for local children's charities. And, spurred on by the fearsome Sir Hugh Allen's Christmas Carol services at Balliol, he had pushed Broadstairs Council into backing a similar one for 1,000 enthusiastic citizens crammed into 'Bohemia', scene of frivolous summer Concert Parties. Even when he was Premier it was a concert which he always found time to conduct. From it came a slender book of words and music, charmingly illustrated, and with a brief introduction to 40 of his favourite carols.

Heath has long promised to write his Memoirs . . . But they are still to appear. Partly perhaps because they could never be as triumphant as 'Music' and 'Sailing'; partly because they would signal the end of a career so nearly of 50 years standing.

Even 40 years back, £6,000 per annum seems a ludicrous salary for a man who had had to sell all his shares at a loss on taking office, and who held our destinies in his hands. Four books in three years did rather better - to the rousing tune of £300,000! Enough to keep him in a succession of ever sleeker, faster 'Morning Clouds'.

Quotation:
'As Prime Minister he angrily refused the seaborne security of a helicopter hovering overhead or of a frigate churning up the waters in his wake. He did agree however to be winched off if political emergency arose. To avoid losing such vital seconds, however, his crew would have preferred simply to toss him overboard in a rubber dinghy!'
John Campbell

HOOKER, Richard (1554-1600)

A Beshrewed Theologian . . .

NO way to be confused with 'Fighting Joe' Hooker, a Gold Rush three-bottles-a-day man with an eye for ladies of easy virtue - who eventually took title from his name. For Richard Hooker was deeply religious and so unassuming that he even doffed his cap to his Parish Clerk. And was 'put out of countenance by his students'.

His father, Roger, though an 'expert, skilful and profitable steward' to Sir Peter Carew could not pay his college fees. Fortunately, Uncle John, a sturdy Devonian, ill-paid Chamberlayne of Exeter for 48 years, and editor of Holinshed's Historical Chronicles (from which Shakespeare took so much) had weight with Bishop Jewel of Salisbury. And as 'a deserving poor scholar', country boy Richard, was dispatched to Corpus Christi, Oxford.

There, it was no easy life. Mere Scholars had to wait upon senior Fellows. The former rose at 4 am; shared a penny piece of beef between four of them for lunch; and at 10 pm walked briskly up and down 'feign to get a little heat in their feet' before retiring to ice-cold beds. Richard, 'an early questionist, a quietly inquisitive boy' became B.A., M.A., Fellow, Regius Professor . . . and, in 1581, ordained priest . . .

. . . a priest so respected by John Aylmer, Bishop of London, that he was chosen to preach at St Paul's Cross, the Hyde Park Corner of those days. It marked a double turning point in his life. Soaked to the skin by an unrelenting downpour, he contracted pneumonia. And was grudgingly nursed through it by his landlord's daughter, Joan Churchman, graceless and ill-favoured and equally ill-tempered, whom nevertheless he married.

As to just why he donned such a hair shirt the pundits vary: out of mistaken gratitude? that he was tricked into it by the girl's father? that he was so shortsighted and short in stature he didn't fully appreciate her ill-looks? Whichever it was, like Socrates, he was married to a nagging, domineering shrew. And yet - 'my dearly beloved wife' was his executrix. Was the 'beloved' merely a final charitable diplomacy?

His sermon however had set him as a key figure at the heart of fierce Church controversy. More, it had persuaded Archbishop Whitgift to appoint him the new Master of the Temple over the head of the ambitious Reader, the Puritan, Walter Travers. Their confrontation turned into a bitter duel between 'pure Canterbury in the morning and Geneva in the afternoon' (when Travers preached). The new Elizabethan Church, lacking a theological and philosophical base, was being torn asunder. To settle the issue, Richard, in 1585, started to turn the spoken word into the written word in his famous book 'Of the Laws of Ecclesiastical Polity'.

But to write it he had to leave the bustle of London; to be given instead a peaceful country parsonage where 'I may see God's blessings spring out of Mother Earth, and eat mine own bread in peace and privacy'. Such peace (wife apart) and privacy he found first at Boscombe in Wiltshire.

He wrote at great length - in majestic sentences and paragraphs. It was no book for the faint-hearted. Yet it was reasoned so cogently and written with 'such sweet language and reasonableness but always with ardour for Truth' that King James, the wisest fool in Christendom, was moved to say 'I have more satisfaction in reading a paragraph of Mr Hooker than in all the long treatises of other learned men. There is no affected language but a clear manifestation of reason'. Even the Pope wrote, 'They shall last until the fire shall consume all learning'.

With four of the proposed eight books written he sought and found still greater peace at tiny Bishopsbourne in the Nailbourne Valley, beneath rolling Downs, near Canterbury. From here he 're-shaped the world' writing much of the remaining books except the last which was unfinished. He was failing in body but his mind still had 'fire, point and pungency'. When, shortly before his death, his house was broken into, his first enquiry was 'Are my papers safe?' Assured that they were: 'Then it matters not for no other loss can trouble me'. Within months of his death his wife had remarried - and as shortly died.

His rectory has been demolished but the yew hedge 250' x 14' x 7' planted by his own hands still grows. In the neighbouring church his portrait bust, showing him in his doctor's robes between pilasters of high-piled books, stands looking down on the ancient altar slab beneath which he is buried.

Quotation:
'But an heretic, by the help of Almighty God, I will never be'.
Richard Hooker

JOHNSON, Hewlett, the Very Reverend Doctor
(1874-1966)

Reddest of Deans . . .

THE man who was to become England's most notorious upholder of Communism was the son of a North Country capitalist.

Dreamy and inattentive as a boy but highly intelligent, and not yet 17, he entered Manchester University, obtaining first a B.Sc., then his A.C.I.E., before dramatically changing course by going to Oxford's Wadham College (where he never rowed in a losing boat) and gaining an Honours degree in theology so that he might become a missionary engineer. Ordination followed - though strangely 'with some reluctance'. His slum missionary work, however, took him only as far as Altrincham, Cheshire, as curate. There, his parishioners were so impressed by his zeal and caring that they unanimously petitioned his Bishop to make him their next vicar . . .

Twenty years later (1924) the Reverend Hewlett Johnson became Dean of Manchester Cathedral. And received sage advice from his grey-haired Head Verger. 'Start with a bang! Get yourself known as the Busy Dean . . . After that, you can slack off'. He did indeed make a loud enough bang to catch the ear of Socialist Premier, Ramsay MacDonald - and Archbishop Lang. In 1931, he landed the plum ecclesiastical position of Dean of Canterbury Cathedral.

It was an appointment which gave him a high publicity platform from which to preach World Peace and World Brotherhood - according to Joseph Stalin. It was also one that gave the Archbishop, the Cathedral Chapter, the Diocese, and indeed the whole country a constant running sore of Conflict.

The trouble was that he equated Communism with Christianity and never hesitated to tell the world so. And the startled world began to feel that this flamboyant prophet must be the Archbishop; a feeling that the Dean himself sometimes shared as he rode highhandedly over his horrified Canons. Villified and traduced by the Press though he was, he fought on.

For the Cause - and to satisfy his own love of arduous and enquiring travel, he toured Russia. There he was gleefully received by a normally sombre Stalin: a propaganda gift-horse had fallen into his lap from on high. It was one so blinkered that it only saw what was good. Astonishingly myopic, the Dean ignored, or apparently did not even notice, Stalin's purges, his concentration camps, his torturing Secret Police, his subjugation of the Orthodox Church, and Lenin's dictum

'Atheism is a natural part of Marxism'. Archbishop Lang, his sponsor, was moved to write angrily: 'You condone what I know is oppression and cruelty'. And to the cynical, Christ Church Cathedral became the Church of St Marx and all Engels.

When England's warm regard for her Russian ally that had fought so heroically and at such cost had sadly turned into the bitterness of the Cold War, it was China that next caught his attention. Fuelled by fanaticism, and 'freebies', he once again travelled enquiringly over vast distances in that huge country and in Central Asia. He worshipped in lamaseries and with the Iman of Tashkent; he was received as joyfully by a more jovial Mao Tse Tung, and Chou-En-Lai, as he had been by Stalin. In all he made five visits - the last when he was still astonishingly fit, physically and mentally, at 90!

Naturally his findings were bruited enthusiastically at home and abroad. He had for many years edited 'The Interpreter' (1905), a religious magazine that was not afraid to look new scientific thought in the face. He was an enthusiastic pamphleteer too. In the depressed 30's, in 'Action Now', he demanded better nutrition for England's malnourished children. In the 50's in 'I Appeal' he fiercely rebutted a House of Lords motion, seconded by his own Archbishop, Geoffrey Fisher, that he be removed, after he had accused America of using germ warfare in the bitter Korean War.

His first book, 'The Socialist Sixth of the World', a Russian panegyric, was launched onto stormy seas. It was published just as that shining example of a civilised country had steam-rollered its way into tiny, neutral Finland, and as Archbishop Lang was praying for it in Canterbury Cathedral with the Dean in attendance. For all that it ran to 22 editions in 24 languages. In this country, Charles Travelyan praised it as 'the best ever book on Socialism for popular consumption'.

'Soviet Success' (1947), the story of his post-war journeyings, became 'Soviet Russia Since The War' in an edition published in America - although he had been refused a travel visa there. His collected sermons in 'Christians and Communism' (1956) sold out in Moscow within seven hours of publication.

In its turn China was eulogised in 'China's New Creative Age' and 'Upsurge of China' (1961). There, as in Russia, he was presented with splendidly bound copies in that nation's language by grateful Heads of State. Their gratitude was also testified by his award of the Stalin Peace Prize and the Star of Mongolia.

Such books, his speeches and his triumphal tours aroused bitter resentment in this country. Red Dean at home appeared abroad to be Head of Church. Archbishop Fisher, who admired him as a man but was diametrically opposed to his views, had angrily to tell New York's cheering dockers, '*I* am *not* the Red Dean'. And when he toured New

Zealand (preaching 98 sermons in 38 days) to save his voice he handed out printed disclaimers to innumerable enquirers. 'The Dean speaks only for himself. He has dominion only over the Cathedral. He has broken no law so he cannot be removed from office'. In fact, he could have been: if he had been unorthodox in his preaching; negligent in his duties; or if, as Johnson himself gleefully pointed out, he'd been not merely immoral (which was sufficient for dismissal of Fellows of All Souls College, Oxford) but *grossly* immoral.

A dragon of a man? No. Infinitely caring - but deluded. His fellow Canons, his Chapter, loathed him; publicly dissociated themselves from him; and regularly petitioned for his dismissal. Even his old friend Canon Crum refused to attend Chapter Meetings that he chaired, or to receive communion from him.

But the people of Canterbury had a soft spot for their 'Red Dean'. It became a term of almost proud affection rather than of opprobrium. After all he was 'a character' with star quality; with timing and his superb voice that disdained modern microphone gadgetry; his piercing blue eyes; his patrician nose; his shining halo of white hair fluffed out on each side of his bald pate; his button gaiters - with their unobtrusive time-saving zip; his briskness and courtesy. 'What an actor! What an exhibitionist the man was!' recalled his left wing publisher, Victor Gollancz.

Before the War he had raised high the Cathedral standard of ceremonial and music. In its early days, he ignored 'It'll be all over by Christmas' optimism and had removed all the Cathedral's heritage of stained glass to underground safety. Tombs of long dead kings and archbishops were sandbagged as massively as a military command post. The 11th century crypt, for centuries past a refuge for Canterbury's citizens, was reinforced. Even a tramway was laid between the towering Gothic piers of the nave so that huge mounds of dry earth could be dumped over the Ambulatory and Choir to soften the impact should the roof above them collapse. During the Baedeker raid the 70 year old Dean (who had just fathered a daughter) walked imperturbably round the Precincts encouraging ARP workers desperately shovelling incendiaries from the Cathedral roof.

When the Blitz was over he gave shelter to the homeless, including an old enemy, in his bomb-shattered Deanery; held record recitals for homesick troops; even entertained General Montgomery (seeking knowledge of what made his Russian allies tick) with his own favourite dish - of grated carrot.

All this was gradually forgotten. When he was 92 his mind was clear enough to write his autobiography, his final task, 'Searching for Light'. But, sadly, when he died just three weeks later, ready to rest at last, and secure in his newly re-inforced certainty of life after death, he was denied memorial service or burial in the Cathedral for which he had fought so hard. Instead he was laid at its heart in the Cloister Garth with his predecessor, founder of Toc H, and wartime padre 'Woodbine Willie' (Dick Sheppard) close beside him.

Quotation:
'. . . blind, stupid, deluded and a public nuisance'.
Anonymous fellow priest.

'A man of heartening courage'.
Actress Sybil Thorndike.

MARCHANT, Bessie (1862-1941)

Teacher Who Told Tales . . .

BESSIE was an ordinary country girl - from remote East Kent - who stood girls' fiction on its head.

Her father was a farmer at Debden Court; her mother, a farmer's daughter. So a love of the land and of the countryside were in her blood. At school, rather grandly named Petham National, she rubbed shoulders (when they were present) with the skivers who willingly sacrificed the joys of the three R's for a penny or two a day picking stones off t' Maister's fields or shaving his hop-poles.

From National she moved on to a private school probably in Canterbury. And so she joined that City's élite band of authors: Christopher Marlowe, Walter Pater, Somerset Maugham . . . not that staunchly traditional King's School went co-ed until the late 1980's. With higher education came an interest in and a facility for writing.

Bessie's birth and the leasing of a second farm at Bodsam Green augured well for Mr Marchant. But he had reckoned without his own Baptist zeal. Elmsted, near his new farm, was known as 'a very dark place, where parents spent the Sabbath in the alehouse' - and children grew up little heathens. For there was neither Church nor Sunday School to reform them. Appalled he set about building a Mission Chapel - which became known as 'The Cathedral in the Woods'.

Such Christian behaviour however found favour with neither Church nor Gentry. The former raised his farm tithes; the latter evicted 'that troublesome Baptist' from Bodsam Farm. It was perhaps an act not totally unexpected from landlord Sir Courtenay Honeywood. He was an obsessive gambler who, unperturbed, had gambled away his own home - and twice won it back in a single night.

Bessie's later education qualified her as a teacher and in appearance she certainly seemed to fit the bill. She was a touch over 6 ft tall, to which she added hair dressed high back on her head. And she wore unbecoming black, as funereal as a priest's cassock, flecked with white only at the neck. Her dominant personality not only forced her pupils to learn but also forced herself each morning, at precisely five minutes past six, - into a cold bath. It was a ritual she observed with all the strictness of the Medes and Persians.

With little prospect of marriage or money in rural Petham she sought and found both in London. In 1889 she married fellow teacher and priest, Jabez Ambrose Comfort. Her writing, in magazines and annuals, was becoming more widely recognised. Eventually, no fewer than 14 publishers, with Blackie taking the lion's share, were to skirmish amongst themselves for her work.

So, in 1898, Bessie happily recorded a literary income of £121 for the year's work. Pride, however, soon took a tumble. Only two years later she was complaining of a 50% decrease. She was sure that it was not that her work was any less well written but that casual editors, unexpectedly and belatedly, returned topical articles and stories which she understood had been accepted. Family finances became so bad that she had to force herself to write to her stepson, asking for a loan of £10. It was a figure which her husband quickly altered to £30!

Her first book, published in 1892 was 'Pease Granock's Father' written with both Kentish scenes and Kentish dialogue. 'Fun of the Fair' had Keston Feast as its centrepiece. 'Yuppie' (surely before its time?) was largely biographical. In 1901, based on her knowledge of Canterbury, came 'In Perilous Times' which dealt with Protestant Martyrdom there by Bloody Mary.

Gradually her approach changed. Not for her, despite her prim and unbending appearance, the conventional books of her day in which Right inevitably triumphed over Wrong. Why shouldn't girls, suffragettes-to-be, have as exciting adventures as did boys? Bessie's longest journey had been from London to Witney where she and her husband now lived. But with the help of assiduous research in Oxford's Bodleian Library, she learnt enough of cannibals and slaves; of wild animals, raging storms and impenetrable jungle vegetation to give her girl explorers a realistic background.

'Held at Ransom' in 1900 and 'Three Girls on a Ranch' in 1901 were breaths of fresh air compared with her predecessor's, L. T. Meade, mawkish goings-on at Lavender Hill School and the saccharine sweetness - of the Headmistress who seemed to take lesbianism in her stride. Came World War I and with it 'A Girl Munitions Worker'. And where 'The Girls' Realm' was still all for cosy domestic bliss, Bessie had strong suffragette sympathies.

She certainly moved with the times and could write as well for boys as for girls. In all she had some 150 books published. And on the completion of each she ceremoniously sang a joyous hymn of thanksgiving.

Quotation:
'Bessie Marchant was the girls' G. A. Henty'.

MARLOWE, Christopher (1564-1593)

Prince of Dramatists . . .

IT was ironic that Marlowe who was to become a notorious heretic and blasphemer, should be born in the shadow of the Mother Church of England, at Canterbury. Ironic too, that the nearby Church of St George the Martyr, where he was baptized, should, in 1942, together with his home, be martyred by Nazi Baedeker bombs.

Ironic too that the man who was to become the prince of Elizabethan dramatists was the son of a mere shoemaker. So, as one of the City's '50 poor boys destitute of help but endowed with a mind for learning', he received, out of the Cathedral funds, a Queen's scholarship to King's School. There the curriculum was Latin, Latin . . . and still more Latin. And there, in Canterbury itself, his innate love for drama must have burgeoned when he saw My Lord Leicester's Players.

Apt in learning he certainly was. After only two years he was ready to move on and up to Corpus Christi, Cambridge. There he lived on a scholarship that allowed him a princely 1/- a week - but where his Buttery bill was 3½d! To his fellows, he was a coxcomb; irreverent, disdaining all convention; and fiery tempered. To his masters, he was 'a rare scholar who made excellent verse in Latin'. By 1583 he had obtained his B.A. degree. Then, for Marlowe, it was London - not the Church for which he was originally destined.

In the capital, the cultured young man with a love of beauty consorted with 'much low company': ruffians, cut-purses and villains. 'Wit lent from Heaven, vices sent from Hell'. Became 'a most subtle searcher of hidden secrets' for Secretary of State Sir Francis Walsingham, for whom knowledge of his parsimonious Queen's hidden enemies was never too dearly bought. To put not too fine a point on it - Marlowe became a spy.

Mere aggression grew steadily into a violent and quarrelsome temper. Two constables were so abused and threatened, that for their very safety they summoned him, unavailingly, to appear before the General Sessions of Peace. In 1592, on a spying trip to Holland he was deported for the issue of counterfeit gold coins. A friend and fellow poet was mortally run through in a brawl that not so 'Kynde Kit' had started. It was to be in another such brawl that he himself was to die.

He played small parts at the Curtain Theatre; indeed 'broke his leg in a lewd scene'. But it was as a dramatists among dramatists, Kyd, Sydney, Peele, Greene that he brought new life and suppleness to the wooden verses of his day. 'All they that love not boys be fooles' he jeered. So though there was beauty in his verses there was little love. Everyday violence tended to become unusual brutality. And the rough and ready humour with which Shakespeare was to amuse the groundlings was seldom for him.

'From jigging veines of rhyming Mother wit
And such conceits as clownage keepes in pay,
We'll lead you to the stately tent of War'.

One unforgettable character bestrode each of his plays. In 'Tamburlaine the Great', a Scythian shepherd became the scourge of God: a man filled with an unbridled ambition to conquer all the nations of the world.

'The monster that hath drunk a sea of blood
And yet gapes for more to quench his thirst'.

His hunger for absolute conquest unfulfilled, he died embittered but ready still to 'Wage war against Heaven itself'.

Barabas, the Jew of Malta, fought, not against the nations of the world but against the Christians of his island who with neither charity nor justice stole his wealth.

'Cellers of Wine and Sollers full of Wheat,
Warehouses stuft with spices and with drugs,
Whole Chests of Gold in Bullion and in Coin,
Besides I know not how much weight in Pearls'.

To regain it, murder followed duplicity, and duplicity, murder - before his inborn treachery led to his own death.

'God-bothering' Dr Faustus, with all the Power of Hell at his command, found that his soul was not bribe enough to the Devil to gain the infinite knowledge that he sought.

'I holde there is no Sinne but Ignorance'.

Marlowe's own death has been attributed to a love affair that went awry; to his avowed atheism; to the need to silence an undercover agent who talked too much . . . But, in plain fact, he was stabbed in a common or garden brawl. One with rascally drinking companions at Widow Bull's inn in the (then) quiet village of Deptford. The dagger that Marlowe, in fury, turned on Ingram Frizer, 'a serving man and rival in lewd love', as he played backgammon, was all too swiftly turned on him - to die, blaspheming and cursing still.

With him there died an unsurpassed wealth of words and imagery; richness of imagination, expression and lyricism. But Kit Marlowe had already paved the way for Shakespeare's giant progress.

Quotation:
'. . . the true Elizabethan blank verse beast, itching to frighten other people with superstitious terrors and cruelties . . . wallowing in blood, violence, muscularity of expression and strenuous animal passion'.
G. B. Shaw

MARX, Karl (1818-1883)

Myopic political theorist . . .

'D as Kapital' was his life's work but certainly not a word he applied to Margate. Although descended from a long line of caring Rabbis he showed neither gratitude for, nor appreciation of the town.

Why should he? Because for four weeks he had received every consideration at the Royal Sea Bathing Hospital. Still, perhaps such grouchiness can be excused when for years you have suffered from - agonising boils. Boils which prevented you from sitting down - even when you most wanted to, in the British Museum Reading Room. Boils that, when London medicine could find no answer, he had treated himself with opium . . . arsenic . . . and creosote! To say nothing of Do-It-Yourself surgery with his own cut-throat razor!

Besides, was not his most fervent 20th century disciple, George Bernard Shaw, to be even more scathing when he described Margate as 'a dismal hole'. Obviously neither of them had ever seen Bank Holiday East Enders' boisterous 'knees-up' outside the town's crowded public houses.

So effective had been the treatment at the Royal Seabathing that Marx (bearded like Zeus himself) descended on Canterbury - after a 17-mile walk. If he had damned Margate with faint praise, he did a demolition job on Canterbury: 'An old, ugly, sort of medieval town, not mended by a large, modern, English barracks at one end and a dry, dismal station at the other. There is no poetry about it. Happily ('happily'? echo a million incredulous tourists) I was too tired and it was too late to look for the celebrated Cathedral'.

Was this his doting wife's 'Schwartzwildschem' (little black wild one) flexing muscle and claw for an attack on the Church: the opium of the people? Be that as it may, surely Marx was as shortsighted in vision as he was eventually proved to be in political economy, if he could not see the glory of Bell Harry towering high above the City.

Buried in upper class Highgate Cemetery in London.

Quotation:
'The workers have nothing to lose but their chains. They have a world to gain'.
Karl Marx

MAUGHAM, William ('Willie') Somerset (1874-1965)

Master of the Short Story . . .

A REMARKABLE man, born, remarkably, on British soil - in the heart of France! That of the British Embassy in Paris. Here his ugly father worked as a solicitor - and adored his strikingly beautiful wife.

So did Willie. Her death, in 1882, from tuberculosis (for which the doctors unavailingly prescribed asses' milk and pregnancy) was a shattering blow. It left him robbed . . . isolated . . . insecure . . . Doubly so when only two years later his father died too.

With a paternal bequest of £150 p.a. Willie was placed in the guardianship of his uncle, the Rev Henry MacDonald Maugham of All Saints Church, Whitstable. The Man of God's first act was to dismiss Willie's last link with security, his Nanny. It became a sound enough reason for Willie to detest him. There were other even better ones ascribed to his uncle by those who knew him well. He was, they agreed: 'Narrow-minded; unintelligent; pedantic; lazy; over-severe; and a cracking snob to boot'. So began the misery and the emotional starvation of the next five years.

Willie lived in a cheerless vicarage. Was forced to wear a velvet knickerbocker-suit with a lace collar - which inevitably invoked taunts of 'Little Lord Fauntleroy'. A parental edict decreed that he should not play with local children. Nor was he encouraged to enjoy Whitstable's sea or beach or bustling harbour. These burdens were borne together with the humiliating stutter of insecurity that was to haunt his whole life.

The only unwitting gift of his guardian was the free run of his large library. In Paris, Willie had been taught English, to match his fluent French, by an eccentric clergyman: one who used murder reports from 'The Times' as his primer. At the vicarage he was able to indulge his longing for a wider range of reading: Scott's Waverley novels, Captain Marryat's breezy sea yarns; Harrison Ainsworth's dark historical novels and, best of all, three volumes of 'One Thousand and One Nights' through which he passed into another world.

Things went from bad to worse. From drear Whitstable vicarage to Canterbury's King's School, oldest in the land; to the bleak Junior department set behind an imprisoning flint wall. Here, frail, knowing nothing of games and this alien way of English life, he was bullied with all the enthusiasm that mindless teenagers can muster. To the latter, his stutter was a Heaven sent gift - even, unbelievably, to some irrascible, impatient teachers. Here, almost friendless in a school of superb buildings set in the shadow of the majestic Cathedral with a clergyman as its Headmaster, Willie did 'four years hard'.

But during them he did become a King's Scholar - with all its accompanying dignity of being able to sport a gown. And now he could counter-attack ruthlessly with a new-found, barbed and wounding wit. He developed too an ever-hardening determination.

A determination to abandon all thoughts of a Cambridge scholarship. Instead 'to go over the wall' before the end of the school year. Then, in the glory of freedom, to travel, to train for a career in medicine which could act as a parachute should his high-flying literary ambitions come to nothing.

So, having steadily worn down his guardians and even his silently worshipped Headmaster's opposition, he headed first for the South of France. Then for Heidelberg University, to study philosophy and literature. And finally for St Thomas's Hospital where, after five years, he qualified, having helped deliver 63 babies in the process. Even more important he learnt the method, orderliness and observation that were to become the foundation stones of the writing he still found time to pursue with relentless purpose.

It was from the nearby squalor of Lambeth (where night walks were perilous unless you carried a black bag) that there sprang his first success: 'Liza of Lambeth'. Too seamy for some it netted him only a disillusioning £20. Still resolute, however, Maugham continued to explore every literary alley until in novel, play, and especially short story he had made his mark worldwide.

Analytically he studied his own craft and that of model prose writers. And thereby learnt his own limitations: 'I have no lyrical quality; no God-given gift of simile and metaphor; no poetic flights of imagination'. But he could tell a gripping story simply and lucidly. It was in 'Cakes and Ale' and 'Of Human Bondage' that he wrote, at his best, of his life in Kent. In successive decades critics tagged him variously 'brutal', 'flippant', 'competent', 'superficial' but he still stands among the literary hierarchy.

Although he hated early rising he helped make his fortune by his ability to write in complete concentration - and isolation. From 6 am to 12 noon! Then, even if in full flow, he switched off. And celebrated with his ritual dry Martini or sweeter White Lady. It was a routine he observed even on a wildly pitching 'Aquitainia' when other passengers - including the famous race-horse Papyrus stabled below decks - were green and prostrate.

It was a fortune that enabled him to buy what was to become the celebrated Villa Mauresque on the Riviera's beautiful Cap Ferrat. Here, above a whispering sea and amid the scent of jasmine and oleander, privileged guests were served cordon bleu dishes - on silver plates - by white-gloved servants. It was a fortune that enabled him to assuage (though never fully) his lifelong wanderlust to the Far East, the South Seas, China . . . It enabled him also to do both small acts of kindness and great acts of generosity.

Very different were Maugham's war experiences which outdid even his own fiction. In World War I, he acted as an undercover agent in Russia seeking to keep that country in the War at any cost. But he was defeated by the Bolshevik coup; and by Petrograd's bitter cold and meagre rations that caused his tuberculosis to flare up again.

World War II began even more dramatically. Germany's lightning Blitzkrieg forced panic evacuation from France for Maugham and 1300 other refugees - in two ageing colliers each designed for a crew of 38! Oran, Petain dominated, denied them sanctuary. So gourmet Maugham, on bully beef, biscuits, and a pint of water a day, was shuttled through skulking U-boat packs via Gibraltar and Lisbon, back to London. It was a two-day voyage - in a hell-ship, that took 20 days and five lives to accomplish!

No military award followed; just as no literary award had yet been vouchsafed him. Indeed, it wasn't to be until 1954 (on his 80th birthday), when homosexuality stank less strongly in Establishment nostrils. And then, it was not the fiercely coveted Order of Merit, (Surely his right?) but the halfway house of Companion of Honour.

Amazingly, through all this, he never forgot the school he had once hated. Now, independent, a legendary character in his own right, Willie could look back on it nostalgically. He became a Governor and visited it - and his guardian's grave - regularly. He gave variously and lavishly. His gifts ranged from a tennis court, and furniture and valuable mezzotints for the Masters' Common Room, to £10,000 for a working class boy's scholarship. Strangely finding no takers it was metamorphosed into a new science block. A library too was built large enough to house the collection of fine books which he had given from his own library.

It is within sight of the famous Norman staircase (where Walter Pater was nearly kicked to death) that, after 91 years, and with his sharp brain sadly dulled by senility, the ashes of Somerset Maugham were interred at his old School.

Quotations:
'Dying is a dull and dreary affair and my advice to you is to have nothing to do with it'.
'I always reserve to myself the privilege of changing my mind. It's the only one elderly gentlemen can share with pretty young women'.
Somerset Maugham

NESBIT, Edith (1858-1924)
A woman of passion: a child at heart . . .

THREE generations of fond mothers have congratulated themselves on finding her seemly but exciting books for their children: 'So suitable, so moral'. They were certain that Edith Nesbit must be a very conventional lady of impeccable repute.

On the latter score how wrong can one be? Although she had been educated at a convent in France, she was audaciously unconventional. She affected gauzy, flowing Liberty's dresses - short hair - beads and bangles - and a long holder for her endless cigarettes. Worse still, she was a radical. And worse still again, a radical who had affaires; affaires with younger men!

On the other hand she adored children. Indeed she was one when she threw herself wholeheartedly into their games and characters. And, no doubt, when she taught fun-loving H. G. Wells and Laurence Housman to play badminton.

At 22 she found herself seven months pregnant, and had to marry Hubert Bland, a monacled philanderer who looked the part. H. G. Wells' assessment was 'A tawdry brain in the Fabian constellation'. Others held him not merely Don Juan but Professor Juan, an ever eager expert in illicit love. One so carelessly enthusiastic that he managed to have two children, over a spread of 13 years, by Miss Alice Hoatson, Edith's closest friend and now the family housekeeper! One of the two, Rosamund, later caught H. G. Wells' roving eye - and probably his roving hands too.

Hubert, however, with Pecksniffian hypocrisy, stlll preached the sanctity of marriage.

Edith accepted both children and loved them as her own. For her part she had four children: was bereft when one died stillborn and was buried in the garden; and when 15 year old Fabian died under anaesthetic - for adenoids! In her turn she also had affaires, generally affectionate ones that helped assuage her well concealed humiliation. She even became infatuated with G.B.S(haw), another womanizer, who enjoyed flirting with so attractive a woman but who eventually rebuffed her eager advances - and was heard to remark, 'Well, at least I didn't say to her, "How dare you?"'.

It was he who best put his finger on it: 'No two people ever married who were better calculated to make the worst of each other'. They did just that for both dramatised scenes, fanning the most trivial quarrels into brief but blazing, door-slamming rows. As Wells wrote: 'They existed in a world of roles, not realities'. And as Edith herself said, stoutly maintaining it was a 99 per cent happy marriage, 'It was my fault. I could have stopped it all. And I didn't'.

At first they had lived at unpretentious, red-brick Halstead Hall situated near to a railway cutting subject to chalk landslips. It was this that gave her the idea for her most famous book 'The Railway Children'. Rather sadly, they moved to 16th century, moated Well Hall, haunted by a spinet-playing ghost. From there, holidays were invariably spent messing about in boats on the placid Medway at Yalding.

That is until she took her children on a mystery tour in a four-horse charabanc . . . Discovered little known Dymchurch. Fell in love with it. Rented a holiday bungalow for the family - and of course for their many friends. For years G. K. Chesterton, Laurence Housman, Enid Bagnold, Hugh Benson and other literary names hurried there at weekends 'to snatch a bed before anyone else seized it'. And to enjoy the Blands' never failing hospitality.

A friend of the poets Rossetti and Swinburne, she was inspired to earn fame rather than pin-money by writing slender verse which, with her aspirations to be a second Shakespeare, she greatly over-valued. When Hubert's ne'er do well partner made off with their capital it was Edith who painted, and wrote verses for Raphael Tuck Christmas cards. And became a literary hack turning out well-structured and characterised pot-boilers.

At first she wrote sentimental adult slop. Then ghost stories including one based on the tomb in Brenzett church of Sir John Fagg. When she found her real metier they were stories of ordinary children - doing extraordinary things; a shrewd mixture of realism and magic. 'The Would-be-Goods', 'The Phoenix and the Carpet', 'The Enchanted Castle', and 'The Amulet' (painstakingly researched at the British Museum where she fell in love with the distinguished curator, Sir E. A. Wallis-Budge, who, mesmerized, advanced, and then beat a shamefaced retreat).

All delighted and intrigued. The 'It' of 'Five Children and It', for instance, was a gawky sand-fairy who granted a wish a day - but only until sunset. It is 'The Railway Children' that is best remembered. It was helped no doubt by regular re-runs of the film in which starred a young, but already delightful, Jenny Agutter. With the story once planned, 5,000 words a day poured from her pen. And she still found time to answer a growing avalanche of letters from young admirers who regarded her as a friend.

When an ailing Hubert, now blind, died, she honestly mourned his passing. But three years later she met Terry Thomas Tucker, a retired marine engineer, bearded like Captain Kettle, and known to everybody as 'The Skipper' . . . Percipient and level-headed, he helped to sort out the chaos into which her home had drifted and where she now lived 'shivering in a sort of Arctic night'. Eventually he told a very lonely Edith 'You look as though you need a tug round here'. And Edith, only too happily, was taken in tow.

Expensive Well Hall was sold. Replaced by two dilapidated but spacious RAF huts which became 'The Long Boat' and 'The Jolly Boat', joined together by a covered way, 'The Suez Canal'. Here life and literature bloomed again until in 1924, bronchitis stealthily but determinedly sneaked up on her. 'Now I am so thin!' she complained. 'Once I was a Reuben's Venus - now I am more like pre-Raphaelite Saint Simeon'. Dying she found was a long business. And, sadly, echoed Frances Cornford's words:

> *'I am so sick, so sick, so sick.*
> *O Death come quick, come quick, come quick'.*

But from her bed, raised by a caring Mrs Thorndike so that she could see out of the window, she wrote:

> *'And see between the Marsh and sky*
> *The little lovely hills of Kent'.*

A tablet in the nearby church of St Mary-in-the-Marsh sums up Edith Nesbit's life: 'I will dwell among my children'. And under the spreading branches of an elm, on a wooden cross made by The Skipper, who had nursed her so caringly, is the single poignant word, 'Resting'.

Quotation:
'Oh little brown brother
Are you awake in the dark?'
Baby Seed Song by Edith Nesbit

ORCZY, Emmuska, Baroness (1865-1947)

Romanticist and artist . . .

A HUNGARIAN girl brought up in Brussels and Paris; knowing Liszt, Gounod and Massenet; trained at a London Art School; and with such a name, seems an unlikely candidate indeed for literary fame in Kent. But it was at Snowfield that she lived and wrote of high romance. Appropriately Snowfield was near Bearsted's equally romantic Green: with its Mourning Tree, a cypress commemmorating 19 year old John Dyke, last man to be publicly hanged on nearby Penenden Heath; and its memories of a Cavalier-Roundhead skirmish.

After exhibiting at the Royal Academy she became well known as an illustrator but real fame came only when, in collaboration with her artist husband, Montague Barstow, she wrote, in 1903, a play - 'The Scarlet Pimpernel'. A romantic public lapped it up. Enjoyed it enough too to buy her book with the same title. Ten more followed including 'Mam'zelle Guillotine' and even a biography, 'A Gay Adventurer', of her fictional hero.

Superficially Sir Percy Blakeney was a fop . . . a dandy . . . an effete and ineffective Englishman. One not worthy to cross swords with Robespierre's ruthless Citizen Chauvelin. But beneath his fashionable clothes there was a master of disguise; a dashing leader who would risk his life time and again to snatch hapless French aristocrats from beneath the guillotine itself. To bring them safely to Kentish shores; perhaps to his favourite staging post, the Rose & Crown in Elham, which still boasts 'good stabling'.

To the adventures of Sir Percy was added the delight of his wife, Lady Marguerite, as beautiful as she was high spirited and resourceful. So lovely indeed that it needed such brightly shining stars as Merle Oberon, Marguerite Leighton and Jane Seymour to do her justice in the films that inevitably followed. She was so fascinating that C. Guy Clayton annexed her as a solo adventuress in his own books.

Sir Percy's film *alter ego* was to be Leslie Howard who years later played the lead role in a not dissimilar World War II drama, 'Pimpernel Smith'.

It was romance, too, that the Baroness loved to create in her own life as well as in her novels. Driving in a carriage and four she revelled in her part of Lady of the Manor and did not hesitate to show her displeasure if girls did not curtsey or boys tug their forelocks in the civility of a past generation as she swept by.

> **Quotation:**
> *'They seek him here, they seek him there,*
> *Those Frenchies seek him everywhere.*
> *Is he in Heaven or is he in Hell*
> *That demned elusive Pimpernel'.*

PATER, Walter Horatio (1839-1894)

Pre-Raphaelite aesthete . . .

PATER was certainly not cut in the heroic mould of his namesake. Bluntly, he was something of a wimp.

He was brought up in the squalor of Stepney, and then, in much more salubrious Enfield. Here his potential was spotted by his headmaster who suggested it would burgeon best in Canterbury - at King's School. Without hesitation, his mother (his father had died of an affection of the brain in 1842) uprooted the family. They moved to Harbledown, the 'Bob-Up-And-Down' of Chaucer's pilgrims, and settled in a Regency terraced house, not far from Lanfranc's Leper Hospital and its Black Prince's Well.

A brave change but a painful one for Walter. Small and frail, precociously pious, neither interested in nor able at games, he became the butt of his much less sensitive fellows. Became not 'the boy most likely to succeed' but 'the boy most likely to be black-eyed'. He could, however, charm, amuse - even shock. And he did have two boyish graces: the wit and the ability to cruelly mimic the Venerable Dean Stanley; and to make realistic animal noises emanate from the mouths of his fellow students at awkward moments.

Thus alienated from the 'muddled oafs' he teamed up, in The Triumvirate, with Henry Dombrain, a hop-farmer's son, and John McQueen. All were equally pious. Indeed Dombrain was known as 'The Archdeacon'; all, where games were concerned, were equally iconoclastic. And those who ate meat during Lent were anathema - to be treated with coldly pointed disdain.

When snow covered Palace Street and the Mint Yard, tradition, and King's was rich in tradition, decreed a battle between Town and Gown. Lacking a cricketer's arm and eye, Pater was relegated to making snowballs for his lustier fellows. And in doing so fell between two stools - pelted by both sides. By his fellows for not making them fast enough: by town louts as the supplier of enemy munitions and, worse still, a King's School toff.

On another occasion, near the gem of the Norman Staircase, he was the butt of what started as good-humoured horseplay but went badly wrong. One boy kicked the prostrate Pater . . . then kicked him again . . . and again . . . His injuries were serious enough for him to need weeks of convalescence. And for his assailant to have been expelled had not Pater generously pleaded for him. For the rest of his life, Pater was to limp.

Even the Headmaster, the mild, much loved Rev George Wallace, also kicked him - only metaphorically of course. On Pater's last day at King's, in 1858, he presented him with a well earned prize; praised his hard work - and then ruined the moment: 'I cannot say you have been an active monitor in suppressing turbulence or punishing the refractory . . .'

Was this turbulence a distant whisper of the rebellion to come under Wallace's successor, Dr Mitchinson who 'Never looked askance at the rod'. Monitors were hissed; missiles hurled at their doors; the Marseillaise sung; and plans made for defending and victualling the Hall to withstand a siege!

Pater himself was equally out of character when he made the traditional leaver's speech, from that same Norman Staircase, to the School assembled below him. The gentle Pater urged them, 'Be boy-like boys'! Just as he later urged Oxford students, 'Burn with a hard gem-like flame'.

Like Hugh Walpole, a hundred years later, he was deeply moved by the Cathedral. 'The very place one is in, its stonework, its empty spaces invade you . . . seem to question you masterfully as to your purpose in being here at all'. Was moved too by the 'dream-like beauty of the City' - not then over-run by tourists and Juggernauts.

With a well-earned scholarship, Pater moved on - to Oxford, to Queen's College, to the life of a scholar. There to become aesthete and critic without peer; and to steep himself in the Renaissance. Oscar Wilde was to eulogise his essay on Leonardo da Vinci (in which Pater described the Mona Lisa as 'one who has learned the secrets of the grave'). And his 'History of the Renaissance' was to become a classic. ·

Pater, with his unmarried sisters, even lived in a style influenced by the pre-Raphaelites. Among his friends he numbered the poets Algernon Swinburne (whom 'Punch' labelled 'Swine Burn' because of his notorious obsession for flagellation), and with Gabriel Dante Rossetti, poet and painter.

Pater became a Fellow of Brasenose and, rather oddly, in view of his monitorial shortcomings at King's School, a Proctor, responsible for University discipline. Here, in his best known book, the philosophic romance 'Marius the Epicurean', he advocated a cultivated hedonism but one allied to strenuous self-discipline.

Oddly, words did not flow as smoothly from his mouth as from his pen. He was as likely to talk of his listener's new shoes as of the Medicis. Even when lecturing, he spoke quietly so much so that when he asked Wilde if he had been able to hear his words, the latter replied, 'Yes, we did just overhear you'.

It is as a stylist that Pater is remembered, one who wrote copiously with an almost enervating wealth of words. 'There', wrote the poet George Moore, 'lies the English language - in a glass coffin'. It was indeed a lying-in-state.

Perhaps Henry James best summed him up: 'Faint, pale, embarrassed, exquisite Pater'. And then damned him with faint praise: 'His style had phosphorescence - but no flame'.

Quotation:
'Mr Walter Pater's style is to me like the face of some old woman who has been to Madame Rachel and had herself enamelled. The bloom is nothing but powder and paint: and the odour is cherry blossom'.
From Samuel Butler's 'Notebooks'

PEPYS, Samuel (1633-1703)

Incomparable Restoration diarist . . . and womanizer

NEITHER Kent- nor aristocratically-born, he was the son of a tailor, the third son of a third son, and a pretty washmaid living in Salisbury Court off Fleet Street. Hardly a likely springboard to a degree at Magdalene College, Cambridge?

Humbly born, but Sam Pepys was to hold audience with the King; dine with dukes and duchesses; become an M.P., President of the Royal Society, Treasurer of Tangier - and Secretary to the Admiralty! (1673). He had brains and ambition - to say nothing of the influential Earl of Sandwich as a patron.

It was his life's work for the Navy that gives us the right to part claim this Londoner for Kent. Regular inspection of the Royal Dockyards brought him frequently into the County and to its numerous north coast ports. Indeed, when the Navy Office was hurriedly moved from Whitehall during the Plague, he actually lived in Kent, at Greenwich, for a time (1665). But he carefully moored his carping young French wife, Elizabeth St Michel (whom he had married when she was barely 15) not alongside in Greenwich but in Woolwich. There, to his shame, he admits, 'I visited her but occasionally'.

And it was at Greenwich that he dreamt his greatest dream! 'That I had my Lady Castlemayne (the King's whore) in my arms and was admitted to all the dalliance I could desire'.

After an inspection at Woolwich (on whose deep waters the mighty 'Harry Grâce à Dieu' and the 'Soverayne of the Seas' had been built) he kept 'a very merry company' at a party to celebrate his wedding anniversary. There he was all eyes, not for his wife ('which made her mad') but for Mercer, her maid, 'who did dance the best jigg I ever did see'.

At Deptford, he drove idling labourers to their work when he went there, officially, to inspect the tarring of ships. Afterwards he dined in highest company: that of the Duke and Duchess of York no less. But for all that he 'skulked off' to visit the ever ready Mrs Bagwell; and Nell, a former maid, with whom he had one bout, and very much, but vainly, hoped for another.

A visit to Deptford was the excuse he gave to his wife when instead he hurried to Lambeth 'and there did what I would with Betty Martin'. The latter's complaisant husband ('a sorry, simple fellow, not worth a farthing'), surprisingly perhaps, rose from lowly Admiralty clerk to Consul in Algiers. And from there he sent a gift to Pepys - a tame lion which, averred Samuel, was 'very good company'.

At Gravesend he was enraged to find, in time of crisis, 'the Duke of Albermarle with a great many idle fops with their pistols and their fooleries'. And at Ham Creek, after a ship inspection, he was much elated by a 13-gun salute from the 'Soverayne'.

Of Dover he had even happier memories for he jubilantly sailed into its harbour with the party who had been deputed to welcome Charles II back from exile in Holland. Sailed in to a crescendo of cheering from a populace rejoicing in a Merry King rather than a long-faced Puritan.

What of the most important of them all - the Chatham Royal Dockyard? It surely harboured some of his happiest and saddest memories. There he taught the Dockyard Commissioner himself how to suck metaphorical eggs by showing him that a single man could carry the baulk of timber for which the former used no fewer than two horses. And there, he wrestled, not unsuccessfully, with the perennial corruption and inefficiency concerning the Chatham Chest, a naval pension fund too often pillaged for less worthy causes.

For all his other tasks there, he found time to visit nearby Rochester Castle: succinctly described two centuries later by Dickens' Mr Jingle, 'Fine place - glorious pile - frowning walls - tottering arches - dark nooks - crumbling staircases'. And it was whilst climbing one of the latter to admire the sweeping view, he hopefully accosted 'three pretty maids and did besarlas muchas vezes et tocar leur mains and necks to my great pleasure'. But, he adds sadly, 'What a terrible thing it is to look down precipices for they did fright me mightily! And hinder me of much pleasure'.

Chatham Dockyard itself held unforgettable memories. Harrowing memories of Upnor Castle safely by-passed; of the Great Chain across the Medway contemptuously cut through; of the 'James', 'Oake' and 'London' all burnt; and, most grievous of all, of the Navy's pride, the 'Royal Charles' with not a man aboard, seized and skilfully towed away at the lowest of water by De Ruyter's able mariners. ('All this whyle King Charles supped with Lady Castlemayne - and chased a poor moth too'). To Pepys such a defeat was more shame than his brief incarceration in the Tower on a trumped up charge of treason. Yet from such ignominy he showed himself at his best in organising an unprecedented programme of shipbuilding to restore the Navy's power - and pride.

His Diaries cover ten momentous years from 1660-1669. They were written in a coded shorthand with bastard French and Italian used to conceal his spicier memories. Written in guttering candlelight until fear that he was going blind brought them to an end.

To Magdalene he left not only the volumes of his Diary but also his unusually diverse library of 3,000 books: all bound in 'decency and uniformity'. The last hundreds hurriedly bought and shipped in trunkfuls to him by friends and emissaries in Europe to reach him just before his death.

A man of wide interests, with a burning love of life, Pepys wrote swiftly, ardently, frankly of the pulsing kaleidescope of London about him. Fresh in language and often witty, his entries seldom stale and no writer has ever described the Great Fire and the Plague more vividly and feelingly.

In Sam's own oft used words: 'And so to bed'.

Quotation:
'Music and women I cannot but give way to'.
Samuel Pepys

RICHARDS, Frank (1876-1961)
(Born: HAMILTON, Charles Harold St John)
'The Chap behind the Chums' . . .

IT was a dog that brought him to Kent. It was Broadstairs' bracing air that gave Billy Bunter another long lease of life. And it doubtless helped Richards to a world record of 72,000,000 typewritten words!

His father was a journalist of sorts whose main delight was in bamboozling officialdom. A true Scot, he was 'Nae mean but car'fu''. That, his addiction to the bottle, and a repressive nature worthy of Mr Barrett of Wimpole Street meant that Charles and his four brothers and three sisters (all christened equally floridly) knew little of freedom, luxuries or treats. So little that on occasion he wished his father dead.

Not surprisingly, he was a shy, self-effacing boy. Precocious too for he early, 'secretly and surreptiously', taught himself the Greek alphabet which he hoped would be the key to his father's library. Equally tenacious in memory, he made himself word perfect in Scott's 'Lay of the Last Minstrel'. And early, he took to scribbling short stories - nowhere more happily than sprawled in a boat.

Before he was 17 he received the first of thousands of editorial acceptances. More to the point, it came with a cheque for £5. This he vaingloriously pinned above his bed rather than cash it. Only for the stonyhearted editor to reduce future ones to £4 after he had met his youthful contributor.

For many, Richards, as he now called himself, and Greyfriars are synonomous but Frank was far from being a one-theme man. The Rio Kid, the boy outlaw, and his mustang 'Sidekicker', and 'Dead Shot Dick' galloped wildly onto the Western Scene. Equally different characters in a different genre were Sedley Sharp, detective,' Len Lex, a schoolboy sleuth - even a spoof Horlock Sholmes. Travel stories, bolstered up by Baedeker and by Peter Fleming's 'Brazilian Adventure', were set even further afield than Frank's own European holidays.

Not that rousing adventures were restricted to dry land. His sea stories included 'Ken King of the Islands', boy skipper of the ketch 'Dawn', trading in the South Seas', blackhearted buccaneers, sea-going dagos, and, believe it or not, Greyfriars 'Remove'! Even Billy Bunter found himself foodless and adrift on a raft. Small wonder that with such wide scope Richards used no fewer than 28 pseudonyms scattered through 47 different magazines. The former ranged from Winston Cardew to T. Harcourt Llewellyn, Ralph Redway to Freeman Fox . . . to Hilda Richards! The latter from 'Ace High Western' to 'Chuckles', 'Dreadnought' to 'Jester', 'Knock-out Fun Book' to 'Detective Stories'.

Equally various were the different schools he created - some 30 in all. Most famous was Greyfriars. For 32 years (1908-1940) the pages of over 1600 'Magnets' bulged with ceaseless escapades, innumerable japes and constant adventures.

Here, never growing a day older, reigned the Remove's Famous Five: manly Harry Wharton who almost outshone George Washington with never a lie throughout; his loyal lieutenant, Frank Nugent, Richards' alter ego; exuberant Bob Cherry; phlegmatic Johnny Bull, the know-all; and Hurre Jam Singh, that splendiferous Nabob of Bhanipur whose ingloriously mixed metaphors and superlative superlatives tore the English language into shreds: 'Their fairplayfulness is terrific'. And - of course - that bespectacled, heavyweight gourmandiser, Billy Bunter, the Fat Owl of the Remove, always scrounging, 'tick' as well as 'tuck'. And often in all too well deserved pain: 'Oh, lor . . . Yaroooh! Help! Yaroooh!'.

Saint Jim's, even with Tom Merry, Gussy, Figgins and Co. was never quite so memorable as Greyfriars. Though it was especially devised to exploit the latter's success for the new magazine, 'Gem', which also never slackened its pace for 31 years.

Boys? All boys? Far from it! Richards was too shrewd an operator not to jump aboard the rolling bandwagon of a growing demand for girls' stories. Bessie Bunter was as obese and as arrogant as her brother; Miss Bullivant, so formidable that with raised and threatening golf clubs she had wrung the women's vote from terrified Cabinet Ministers; wholesome Marjorie Hazeldene was the 'rippingest' of girls.

Then there was her tomboy friend, Clara Trevlyn, ever eager to 'make things hum'. Fearlessly she challenged sexist Bulstrode to a fight - confident, in her woman's duplicity, that he would be too gentlemanly to strike her, and that even if he did, she could turn on floods of disarming tears.

Never have so many young readers owed so much to one author. Blind and deaf to interruption, Richards wrote for nearly 70 years. In that time he tapped away ceaselessly at his old Remingtons with their violet ribbons at a steady 50 words a minute. It was 18,000 in a day if he utilized his self-devised Heath Robinson milk-drip and, when painfully cramped, limbered up on garden parallel bars originally installed for his young eight year old niece, Una. 100,000 in a busy week. And 72,000,000 words, far more than those of any other known author, in a lifetime!

Not that all was plain sailing. Came World War I. With paper in very short supply, both 'Gem' and 'Magnet' ceased publication. At a stroke his income of £2,500 a year was almost decimated. And unfeeling, retrospective Tax Claims still rolled in. Undeterred, although nearly 40, in true Greyfriars style he suddenly stamped out of the house to enlist - only to find the Recruiting Office closed. A second, rather less impulsive attempt, resulted in his being categorised as 'Totally unfit for War service'.

It was War - and a dog - that brought Richards to Kent. Mickey had 'found' him in Marseilles - and refused to let go. And he was with him in France in mid-August 1914 when Richards headed desperately for Dieppe - and England. The latter escaped the steadily closing German net but officialdom refused Mickey passage. On landing at Folkestone, his first thought was to find temporary lodging - at Hawkinge Post Office - so that he could make a quick sortie (to be delayed for four years) across the Channel to regain Mickey. Meantime he had bought Clyde Cottage. And later built 'Apple Trees' as a 'holiday home', both in Hawkinge.

With the War over he dispatched his housekeeper to Thanet to find a house where Una could enjoy sun and bracing air. She chose 'Rose Lawn', a gabled villa in Percy Avenue, Kingsgate, that overlooked cornfields and the sea. There he was to spend the last 40 years of his life, strangely, slowly changing from ardent traveller to obsessive recluse.

In a World War II Defence Area he was eventually forced to leave 'Rose Lawn' and its large vegetable patch that he had patriotically 'Dug for Victory'. By 1945 he was back again. So too was Bunter. Moving up the literary ladder he no longer appeared in 'Penny Bloods', a term Richards hated, but in hardback. Over 38 of them and all with 'Bunter' in the title. In 1952 the latter made his T.V. bow - as low as his waistline and tight-fitting trousers permitted. Richards' fortune, not at his own suggested 30/- a thousand words but on a much more generous editorially decreed royalty basis, was on the up again.

Life generally was 'on the up' until he was savagely attacked in a 'Horizon' diatribe by George Orwell, recent author of 'Animal Farm'. He accused Richards' work of escapism, snobbishness, élitism, zenophobia, even sadism. After all Form Master Quelch was all too frequently depicted, quivering cane raised on high, administering not six of the best but up to 30 to the Bunter posterior. 'It all' growled Orwell, smacked of 'the mentality of a rather stupid member of the Navy League in 1910'.

Outraged, Richards sprang to his own aggressive defence. He made no bones that he admired the old-fashioned virtues; that he gave enormous and harmless pleasure to millions; that he preached the virtues of truthfulness, friendliness and loyalty. Admittedly, he did raise the black demons of betting, smoking and gambling but it was only to knock them down as sheer folly. And he skirted round sex with all the delicacy of a maiden aunt. Even so, an Ipswich librarian could still rubbish him for ridiculing unhappy fatties such as Bunter and Turkey Tuck. As a result Bunter found himself relegated (not unwillingly?) amongst the sex books in the discreetly sited 'Reserved Section'.

Undeterred by this fracas, he and his aged Remington rattled happily on. Skull cap replacing unsuccessful and insecure toupé, swathed in a dressing gown, with his trousers tightly bicycle-clipped, he peered over his heavily inked manuscript with the help of thick spectacles and magnifying glass.

Wisely, he had never allowed such robot labours to preclude pleasure. Quite early he had become an inveterate Channel-hopper. An even more inveterate compulsive gambler whose cascading royalties long did much to sustain Continental casinos, especially those at Le Touquet and Monte Carlo. Even amid the beauty of the Italian Lakes or the magic and mystery of Pompeii he had to work for three or four hours a day to keep up with his relentless weekly schedule: three 20,000 'worders', a dozen freelance articles. Pipe smoker, scholar, he read and translated Latin classics; published 'Ultio Bunteri' in the prestigious Times Educational Supplement, and even translated 'Waltzing Matilda' into Roman vernacular.

Richards died peacefully in his sleep on Christmas Eve; and was borne over skating-rink roads amid swirling snow to Charing Crematorium. For nearly 70 years his enthusiastic, runaway pen and fecund imagination had brought warmth into millions of young lives.

Quotation:
'Never have so many youngsters owed so much to a single author'.

ROCHESTER, John Wilmot, 2nd Earl of (1647-1680)

Poet - and rake . . .

TRUE, an Oxfordshire man . . . but admitted to these Kentish pages on three counts: (a) A nearish neighbour; (b) One too wicked to omit; (c) An undeniably Kentish title.

The ermine cloak of 2nd Earl fell upon his narrow shoulders when he was only 11. The future was to show that he had inherited much from his father - and very little from his mother. The former had been a dashing Cavalier; the latter a devout Puritan. A Master's Degree at 15 at Wadham College was followed by a leisurely three-year Grand Tour with an easy-going tutor.

At 18, inspired perhaps by continental beauties, he returned to scatter the eager suitors of Elizabeth Malet, as rich as she was beautiful. And to abduct her in worthy style - in a resplendent coach drawn by six powerful horses. It took 18 months of protracted negotiation (some of it spent incarcerated in the Tower) before the Malets would agree to the marriage. To while away the rest of the time, he fought at sea against the Dutch and showed conspicuous courage.

Once married they settled at his birthplace, Woodstock Park, where Aubrey delights to tell us 'He had several lascivious pictures drawn'. Elizabeth spent much of her life there rearing her four children. Rochester, a talented cavalier, more frequently headed for London on the outskirts of which he maintained 'There the devil enters into me'.

There too his good looks, easy manners, quick mind and still quicker tongue made him a 'Court wit', the King's boon companion and a Groom of the Royal Bedchamber. Frequently he overstepped even the most generous mark . . . was banished . . . only to be as swiftly missed and recalled. Even in Charles II's epitaph, Rochester pulled no punches:

'Here lies our Sovereign Lord the King
Whose word no man relies on
Who never said a foolish thing
Nor ever did a wise one'.

It was such but far more biting lampooning that roused a fellow sufferer Sir Car Scroope to write:

'Sit swelling in thy hole a vexed toad
And all thy pox and malice spit abroad
Thou canst blast no man's name by thy ill words
Thy pen is full as harmless as thy sword'.

There too he could, with his dissolute fellow revellers, create drunken debauch and riot. There too he could enjoy his strumpets, and his mistress, Elizabeth Barry, from whom he had swept aside poor besotted Otway. 'Poor Otway' who, having first set Elizabeth's ungrateful foot upon the stage in his 'Alcibiades', had hoped for better things. But to be fair to Rochester, he did write as frequently to his wife when with his mistresses as to his mistresses when with his wife.

Rochester was a patron of poets as well as of prostitutes. But even Dryden's flattering avowal: 'You can write better on the meanest subject than I can on the finest' did not prevent him being beaten up by Rochester's bully boys when he was suspected, wrongly, of writing a humiliating lampoon about him. The biter bit indeed! And when a certain Mr Pordage, having left his 'Herod and Marianne' for the Earl's approval, he received on his return, not congratulatory encomiums but a terse couplet:

> *'Poet, who ere thou art, God damn thee.*
> *Go hang thyself - and burn thy Marianne'*

'Profligate', 'Atheist', 'Obscene Versifier', 'Drunken Rake': Rochester's Press was hardly one to boast about. (Though admittedly a kindlier critic asserted that he probably did have 'some amiable qualities'). Bawdy he was in verse as well as in life. Indeed he wrote more unequivocally about sex than anyone else until the 20th century. And yet he could write graceful, unblushing lyrics; imitate both Horace and Boileau; and produce 'Verses to Lord Mulgrave' and 'Verses to Nothing'. His 'A Satire Against Mankind' was most skilfully and logically developed:

> *'. . . one of those strange prodigious creatures Man . . .*
> *I'd rather be a Dog, a Monkey, or a Bear*
> *Or anything but that vain animal*
> *Who is so proud of being rational'.*

Even Dr Johnson, no prude, insisted that Rochester's bawdier verses be 'castrated' before appearing after his (Johnson's) Preface. And his editor, Dr Taylor, in a rare burst of humour, remarked that had Rochester himself been castrated such poems would never have been written.

Such dissipation and its consequent disease made its ugly mark. Little over 30, Rochester was already dying - and, with all his old intensity, desperately seeking a deathbed conversion. In this he was much helped by Gilbert Burnet, a scholar so highly regarded that he had been able to refuse four Bishoprics before he was 29. (But later had his pastoral letter supporting William III burnt by the common hangman).

It was by his help that Rochester could summon his entire household, down to the youngest swineherd, to hear his deathbed repentance. One so touching that when Burnet wrote his 'Life of Rochester', Dr Johnson was moved to say 'We have a very good Death but there is not much Life'.

Quotation:
'Rochester blazed his Youth in lavish voluptuousness' Dr Johnson

ROOK, Jean (1931-1991)

First Bitch of Fleet Street . . .

JEAN ROOK was big, blonde, busty and overbearing. She was filled with a zest for living, an ambition to be the best. It was one that rode roughshod over other people's feelings. With ambition went a near suicidal willingness to undertake any stunt she or her editor devised. Jean Rook had guts.

She owed her rocket-ride to the top to three things. An observant eye for detail. A thick streak of iconoclasm which enabled her happily to debunk even the greatest. And a style of writing like a Brock's benefit night where startling similes and metaphors sparkled in every sentence. 'She wrote as brightly as the jewelry she loved. 'Penny plain' was certainly not a maxim to which she subscribed. 'Tuppence coloured' was. A reader emerging from a Rook article felt as brain-battered as a Mike Tyson victim is body-bruised.

The War intervened to prevent her going to Roedean. Instead it was Hull's Malet Lambert G.S. and, during the War, Westerdale village school, and Whitby G.S. for her. She travelled to the latter by the North Yorks Moorland Railway - often suspended by her heels from the luggage rack. With her brain surprisingly unimpaired by such mode of travel she settled for four good A Levels but flunked entry to both Oxford and Cambridge; and set sail for London University's Bedford College.

There, 'Big-boobed, big-bottomed, short-waisted, 5' 7½" and 13 stone' (her words, not mine!) she indulged in hard work, the pleasures of the Town, and the heady delights of young men. And, finally, when bribed by her much loved father with a second-hand car, she put in 18 months hard research in the British Museum's Reading Room to achieve a Master's Degree in English Literature.

Academia behind her she eagerly settled for the real world. After summary rejection by the Hull Daily Mail she certainly found it with the Sheffield Telegraph. Under the uncompromising Ernest Taylor, 'The Barnsley Bull', she learnt her trade in a hard school. And met her future husband, Geoff Nash - destined always to be just another Agency reporter.

From Sheffield, Jean Rook climbed the Fleet Street ladder faster than a circus acrobat. At 'Flair' she started by successfully crossing swords with top model, Tania Mallet. In 1964, very Welsh Hugh Cudlipp, reputedly 'a fiery sexual dragon', enticed her to 'The Sun'. There, Amy Landrath, the Woman's Editor, despite an upbringing at Cheltenham's genteel Ladies College, was 'hell on high heels'. And there Jean failed to scoop the story of a skeletal 6 stone 16 year old . . . Twiggy.

David Essex of the 'Daily Sketch' though 'morally as stiff as his moustached upper lip' had no scruples about offering to double her salary. So she joined him just in time to give zip to his 'Save the Mini-

Skirt' campaign. New tabloid 'Mail' swallowed 'Sketch' - just as Jean found herself pregnant. 'They can share a birthday cake' quipped her new editor, David English.

One rung left to climb! Within 18 months 'muck mean' John Junor of the 'Express' had three times outbid the Mail in its quest for her scarifying pen. Jean Rook the first - and highest paid columnist in Fleet Street - was to hold sway in the black glass Lubianka of the Express building.

She feared no one. The higher they were, the harder they fell. And the insatiable public loved it. Royalty was a prime target. Prince Philip was denounced as 'a snappish OAP with a temper like that of an arthritic Corgi'. Fergie was labelled both 'a Frump and a Disaster Area'!

Mary Whitehouse was 'a whited sepulchre who had awarded black marks to films she had only dared watch through half-closed fingers'. 'Whingeing' Germaine Greer, a self-appointed sexpert, was written off as 'intensely dreary'.

Lesser lights, such as the Archbishop of Canterbury, Dr Runcie, got away with 'that ineffectual old bleater who's no use down here'. And Arthur Scargill was denounced as 'willing to call out his own shadow on a nod'. Almost alone, 'Wonder Woman' Margaret Thatcher was spared the lash.

Such killer attacks needed no bravery. But despite the title of her autobiography Jean Rook was certainly no 'Cowardly Lioness'. She had been hoisted 120' high to Olympia's roof at the Boat Show; 'trained' man-eating tigers in public alongside Mary Chipperfield; been the 'target' of motor cycle stunt man Eddie Kidd who, with his 14 stone Yamaha, roared 6" above her head.

In her personal life she was braver still. Though terrified, she had faced up to breast cancer and 'the Dante's Inferno that is chaemotherapy'. Faced it, since she had long moved from Petts Wood pseudo-Gothic to West Kent 7-bedroomed hilltop mansion, at Pembury General Hospital and her own Edenbridge Cottage Hospital.

Only six months after recovery she was roughly awakened to see baleful eyes glaring at her through balaclava slits; and to hear 'Do as I tell you or I'll kick your f*****g face in' And then be dragged crashing down the stairs to the hall. To watch gold souvenirs from her worldwide travel disappear into the night.

To watch, too, her husband's equally traumatic treatment. And for three years after to watch and care over his gradual disintegration until an inoperable brain tumour plunged him into terrifying dreams. He died on their 25th Wedding Anniversary.

Even her baby boy was marred with astigmatism. Astigmatism so bad that at 8 months he could see only a blurred world and had to wear ludicrous five penny piece-size lenses across his button nose.

Few people could have suffered more but Jean Rook came up still fighting, still feisty; still able to write a punchy article for her millions of avid readers.

Quotation:
'You're too old. Over-educated. You haven't a cat in hell's hope of Fleet Street'.
Editor of the Hull 'Daily Mail'

SACKVILLE-WEST, Victoria Mary (1892-1962)

Novelist, Poet - and Creator of Gardens . . .

AS a daughter of the 3rd Baron Sackville, her ancestry was rich in romance. Her great-grandmother, Catalina Ortega, had scraped a hungry living in Spain by taking in washing and selling old clothes. Her grandmother, Josefa Duran, 'Pepita', had been a famous exotic dancer. And her mother, Victoria, temperamental and totally unpredictable, was the offspring of Pepita and an English Milord, Lionel Sackville-West. From such a mixed lineage Vita rose phoenix-like to make her name among the Bloomsbury literary élite.

Her home background was even richer and more romantic. Knole was a 15th century Archbishop's Palace containing a little matter of 365 rooms, 52 staircases and 7 courtyards - one which Henry VIII had seized, without so much as a by your leave, from the unfortunate prelate. Today it holds pride of place in Kent's National Trust. During her childhood, Vita roamed over it from cellars to long-forgotten attics; from muniment rooms to glittering royal staterooms; from the Great Staircase with proud leopards on newel posts to Retainers' Gallery where she found sanctuary when sulking.

There, as a young child, she showed an early masochistic streak: equally small guests were tied to trees and their bare legs beaten with nettles! Until she was 13, and now much more civilised, she was taught by relays of governesses necessitated by her mother's sharp tongue and quick temper. Despite such changes she became an omnivorous reader and a prodigious writer. Eight historical novels (her day-dreams) and five plays, three in French, rolled smoothly from her pen before she was 18.

And it was from Knole that she wrote the first of thousands of letters (duly published) to 'Dear Mr Harold' (Nicholson). And there, of course, in 1913, she was married in a tiny chapel before just 26 close friends - whilst 400 more waited impatiently outside for the reception. It was a famous (infamous?) enduring marriage in which 'Mr Harold' indulged his homosexual proclivities and she her lesbian ones.

But such affaires are not our business here. Except perhaps that with fellow author Virginia Woolf whose remarkable and readable 'Orlando' was a thinly veiled portrait of Vita. It was, Vita's son wrote, 'the longest and most charming love letter in literature'.

In her thirties, Vita's wide-ranging pen was nearly as prolific as in her teens. 'The Land' (1927), a Georgic poem, captured the atmosphere and rhythm of Kent rural life - captured also the rather conservative Hawthornden Prize. Twenty years later, with a £100 Heinemann Prize for 'The Garden', she beautified Sissinghurst's Moat Walk with a vivid display of azaleas. And in it made even fertilizers poetic!

> '. . . a grudging soil
> Enriched or lightened following its need;
> Potash and compost, stable-dung, blood, bone,
> Spent hops in jade-green sacks, the Autumn leaves
> Rotted and red, the wood-ash from the hearth'.

Her prose was more varied; and she wrote particularly evocatively of her travels. Vividly she described her honeymoon home - and the first garden she created: an idyllic suntrap, wooden house surrounded with pomegranates, and pergolas heavy with grapes, overlooking the minarets of Santa Sophia and the Golden Horn below. She wrote equally vividly in 'Passenger to Teheran'. There her husband was Chargé d'Affaires - and she assisted at the coronation of the Shah. (The latter she labelled 'bedint', the contemptuous Sackville cult word for common - and therefore lower class).

Equally excitingly she described the dangerous trek through the wild Bakthiari Hills and her return to England through a gloom-ridden, terror-filled Russia. 'Compulsive reading. A splendid lovely book' purred her proud husband. 'Knocks all others into a cocked hat'.

People too she reincarnated: Aphra Benn (qv), Kent's Restoration spy and dramatist, two St Theresas, and Joan of Arc - all women of her own fiery spirit. And in 'Pepita' she brought alive her grandmother just as in 'Knole and the Sackvilles' she captured the spirit of her forbears and her beloved home. Beloved, but because she was a woman, never to be hers. It was a loss that rankled all her life.

Her novels were not so successful. 'Dragon in White Water' was as odd as its title. A bizarre and violent story of bizarre and violent people. It ended with a blind man hurling a deaf-mute into a vat of boiling soap. 'Challenge' (1923) had to be withdrawn just before it was bound as its heroine was too patently her lover, Violet Trefusis, daughter of one of Edward VII's longer lasting mistresses. 'The Edwardians' depicted the luxury and sumptuous way of life of the smart set in that same era.

Vita and Harold had turned Long Barn, near Sevenoaks Weald, into a house and garden of distinction. Seeking a new challenge they bought, for £12,375, the tattered ruins of Sissinghurst Castle: 16th century Elizabethan Palace of 'Bloody Baker'; 18th century French Prisoner of War camp; 19th century Poor House; 20th century rubbish dump. And succeeded triumphantly in turning seven acres of muddy wilderness into a Kentish Paradise.

This unfortunately is no place to describe her creation of original, small, self-contained gardens within a garden: gardens of a single colour or for a single season; gardens, sometimes of exuberance and extravagance yet wholly of Kent and England. 'It's like being made a Fellow of All Souls' she crowed when she was awarded the R.H.S. Veitch Gold Medal.

'No place' - except that the garden showed Vita at her best. And that over it soared the turretted tower which she had straightway appropriated, as her right, as a study.

'Here, tall and damask as a summer flower,
Rise the brick gable and the springing tower'.

In it, for over ten years, she weekly wrote 'those beastly little articles': 'Gardening Notes' for the Observer (at 15 guineas a time) which elicited much praise; praise which she described as 'neither deserved nor desired'.

And it was at Sissinghurst that she died, in the Priest Cottage - on a day perfect for gardening. Her last words were spoken to a favourite retriever. And her bed was covered by Harold with flowers from the garden which she had so lovingly created and described so evocatively in prose and verse.

Quotation:
'She looks like Lady Chatterley above the waist - and her gamekeeper below'.
Cyril Connolly

SMART, Christopher (1722-1771)

Madman and poet . . .

BORN and reared in rural Shipbourne, near Tonbridge, the son of Sir Harry Vane's steward. On going up to Cambridge he became an outstanding classical scholar. A poet too who wrote feelingly and knowledgeably of the county in 'The Hop Garden'. An immensely long and detail-packed Georgic effusion: a veritable 18th century DIY textbook on Kent's centuries' old expertise.

Unhappily, improvidence and a secret marriage that failed wrecked what might have been a brilliant career. Dr. Johnson, who took Smart under an unusually protective wing, recorded that the poet gradually had only half his quota of necessary exercise. For although he strode purposefully enough through crowded London streets to the nearest tavern - he invariably had to be carried back home.

Not only a drunkard but also a religious fanatic! All too slavishly he followed the Lord's injunction to 'pray without ceasing'. He did just that by night and by day; pestered his friends at the most inconvenient moments to join him; and regularly fell on his knees in crowded streets passionately urging startled passers-by to follow his example.

The poet was certified mad. Was put away. But Johnson defended him fiercely. 'His infirmities were not so obnoxious to Society. In every other transaction of man's life he could not have been more regular. I would have lief have prayed with Chris Smart as any man'. And yet when asked whether Smart or Derick was the better poet he replied with his usual brutal frankness, 'One does not make distinction between a louse and a flea'.

For a time (in 1756) Christopher was freed from the horrors of an 18th century asylum. And in his freedom wrote his best known poem 'Song to David'. Tetchy Dr Burney thumbed his way briskly through it. 'As mad as ever' was his verdict. Robert Browning's was very different: 'In structure and in imagery, it is like a great cathedral'.

> 'For I will consider my cat Jeoffrey
> For he is the servant of the Living God, duly and daily servicing him.
> For at the final glow of the Glory of God in the East, he worships in his way.
> For this is done by wreathing his body seven-times round with elegant Quickness.
> When his day's work is done, his business properly begins
> For he keeps the Lord's Watch in the night against the adversary;

For he counteracts the Powers of Darkness by his electrical
skin and glintirg eyes;
For he counteracts the Devil who is Death by brisking about'.

Not so mad, surely?

Quotation:
'Glorious the Northern Lights ashine;
Glorious the song when God's the theme;
Glorious the thunder's roar'.
'Song to David'

SWING, Captain

Laconic bloodcurdler . . .

NO one single man but a composite of scores of Luddites not only in East Kent but also in most of England's southern counties. Lower Hardres near Canterbury was the scene of the first night attack then Brasted, Borden, Selling Court . . . and, eventually, virtually the whole of the South was aflame.

In the 1830's, the Starvation Years, parsons waxed fat and comfortable on tithes. Stonyhearted magistrates ordered 'Transportation to the Antipodes' without a flicker of compunction. Farmers treated and housed their labourers with less concern than they gave their cattle. And now, crushingly piled on that, they were eagerly buying the newly invented threshing machine: a monster that denied winter work to hungry farmhands.

Small wonder that Captain Swing was never short of recruits. With bludgeons and blackened faces, they marched purposefully with him at dead of night. In minutes they could smash one of these machines into pieces, or turn a farmer's rickyard into a crackling inferno.

Few men have written less with such lack of literary skill but with so fearful an effect as did Captain Swing. More at home with a sledgehammer in his hands than a pen, he wasted few scrawled words:

'Your name is down among the Black Hearts. And this is to advise the likes of you who are Parsons, Justices, Farmers to make your Wills'.

'If you don't rise the poor man's wages, we'll burn down your barns - and you in them'.

'You have by grinding system and grudging economy wickedly thrown your labourers into the Poor Law'.

'We are 5,000 men - *and will not be stopt!'*

Repression was savage: 20 hangings, 500 transportations, countless imprisonments and evictions, peaceful protesters routed by hardbitten Dragoons. But so widespread was the revolt, so great, public sympathy, that sheer weight of numbers told.

Captain Swing became King Ludd; farm labourers gleaned a better living.

Quotation:
'Tis the wreckers should be burnt - not our barns!'.
Uninsured Farmer

TERRY, Dame Ellen Alice (1848-1928)

Lady of Letters . . .

NO, you have not mistakenly picked up a 'Who Was Who Of The Stage'. Ellen Terry was undeniably the darling of the theatre during three reigns. She was also a skilled and prolific letter writer, capable too of well-written 'Memoirs' (1908).

For 26 years she more than held her own in a paper-passion correspondence without equal. It was with the greatest dramatist of her day - the fiery Irish genius, George Bernard Shaw. And yet for nearly ten years they studiously avoided a personal meeting. (Even on tour she sometimes wrote 30 letters in a day - many to people who had asked her help).

She was born not with a silver spoon in her mouth but a property one. Born into a remarkable theatrical family - 13 strong. She was just 8 when she made her West End theatre debut as Mamilius in The Winter's Tale, and in panto, as Fairy Goldenstar. Farce, burlesque and melodrama were to follow. During her teens she was coached so well by Charles Kean that her every word rose, clearly and hauntingly, even to the very back of the Gallery. 'She had a voice of plum-coloured velvet' wrote James Agate.

At 16, Ellen was married briefly, innocently, to the artist G. F. Watts, 27 years her senior, who swore, falsely, 'I could paint you for ever'. They parted within a year. At 20, this time desperately in love, she married Edwin William Godwin, an architect, as unfeeling as his raw materials and unfortunately much more mobile. For six years (1868-1874) she sacrificed her bright career to run his household on £3 a week, and to bear two children. When Godwin's behaviour became unbearably erratic she was, by a chance meeting, and by penury, enticed back to the theatre by impresario Charles Reade (author of "The Cloister and The Hearth").

Within four years Henry Irving, idol of the English stage, had annexed her as his leading Shakespearean lady to play her greatest role, Ophelia. In love perhaps, but not lovers, there's was a bewitching partnership that was to last for nearly 25 years and make her a living legend.

Her dramatic triumphs in this country and on 10 American tours have, sadly, no direct place here. It is her amazing 'love by letter' saga that intrigues us. It too began by sheer chance. In 1892 when she was 44 and married, ever caring, she wrote to the Editor of 'The World' seeking professional guidance for an acquaintance, Elvira Gambogi, a singer. Much less caringly it was casually tossed to the new 38 year old music critic who also wrote plays and was an impassioned Socialist - George Bernard Shaw.

His letter was professional but stiff and formal, without warmth or character. Only his much more uninhibited reply to her 'Thank you' sowed the seed from which flowered hundreds of fascinating and intimate letters of self revelation - written as if spoken, and with no thought of publication or meeting.

Early in their correspondence (1895) Shaw made it plain that it would not be that of a curate and deaconess in a small country town. And although Ellen's letters might begin staidly enough 'Oh, dear GBS, how do you do?' or 'Dear Mr Conscience' or even 'Old Stupidest' they would end with 'Blessings on your dear head', 'Oh, I am very much yours', 'Your lover, Ellen'. The words of a wife? And yet not for nearly a decade did they actually meet!

Where lay the attraction? Initially each doubtless was intrigued by the other's reputation. Physically, Ellen, tall, blue-eyed and blonde, was the beauty of her day. Shaw, on the other hand, described himself as 'a disgracefully cruel-looking middle-aged Irishman with a beard'. And with 'ears that stick out like the doors of a triptych: a Shaw speciality'. .

GBS was a compulsive womaniser who once had six ladies in tow at the same time, but seldom overstepped the sexual mark. As to Ellen, his high regard and deep tenderness for her made him determine that he would not allow his 'ridiculous philandering' to ruin their relationship. Ellen on her side did marry three times. Here, for both of them was safe and leisurely flirting. Safe as long as they didn't meet - only to be disillusioned or to rub the bloom off their friendship. (For him, intellectual passion transcended physical passion as was the case when he eventually married 'his green-eyed Irish lady with millions' - and 'volcanic tendencies'. Married her without a quibble even though she had decreed 'No consumation'!)

GBS was delighted and amazed to find a sensitive intelligence in so beautiful an actress. Naturally many of their letters were of stage and drama, of plays and people, of production as well as acting. Each learnt and gained from the other. Ellen was experienced and intelligent enough to put her finger on flaws in GBS's arguments, to tell him when a play had passed its sell-by-date, or which young actress he should best approach to take a certain part in his latest drama.

Shaw for his part wrote plays for her, even an 'Intelligent Actresses Guide to Cymbeline'. And deliberately but unsuccessfully used Ellen as intermediary in his sometimes bitter struggle to persuade the all too Conservative actor-manager, Henry Irving to stage one of his modern plays. Together, GBS and Ellen revelled in the duelling of intelligent, witty, charming and caring pens.

Her letters reveal her love of her own cats and dogs; hatred of cruelty to circus animals; abhorrence of the death sentence imposed on Annie Ansell for the murder of her sister; the joy she had from her secluded cottages at Smallhythe and Winchelsea, from touring the Marsh in her jaunting car, and from canoeing peacefully on Pitt's Royal Military Canal.

They drew too a vivid picture of a mother who loved her extravagant children 'much more than myself'; of her caring for others; of paralysing first night nerves; of overwork and illness: 'tired out', 'half dead'; of recurrent trouble with her overworked eyes.

ET and GBS grew to know each other's very selves . . . and deliberately avoided meeting for fear of breaking the spell. Shaw had, earlier stood beside her in a jostling audience but Ellen, deep in her own thoughts, had not recognised him. As a drama critic he had of course seen her frequently - and with enchantment - on the other side of the footlights. Whilst she had seen him only once or twice, momentarily, through the stage-curtain peephole.

Gradually the flame glowed less brightly . . . Then, in 1906, she read his arrestingly titled 'Captain Brassbound's Conversion'. In it he had written the part of Lady Cicely Waynflete 'to fit her like a glove'. Ellen turned it down - flat. 'I don't like the play one bit. It simply won't act'. And yet later, after seeing a scratch rehearsal, she capitulated handsomely: 'I adore it' and played in it.

It was during rehearsals for that play that she and Shaw did at last meet. But her failing eyes were more on James Carew, the handsome American leading man, than on Shaw. Setting all canvas, she sailed across the room, anchored alongside, and swept off with her prize almost before he knew who or what had hit him. It was however a short-lived marriage for youth and sexagenerian jealousy are poor bedmates. James Carew was soon 'painlessly dispatched'.

Alas, in person, Ellen and GBS could not sustain the rapport created by their pens. So, slowly, the fervour of their correspondence abated. Dozens of letters each in a year became two or three; two or three might even dwindle to none for 12 months. But their affection lived on. And after her death at Smallhythe, near Tenterden (now the National Trust

Ellen Terry Museum) where she had lived for many years, was found a long list of 'My Friends'. In it, GBS stood high - unchallenged except by Charles Reade who had started her amazing career anew.

Quotation:
'One may say that her marriages were adventures and her friendships enduring'.
G. B. Shaw

THORNDIKE, Arthur Russell (1885-1972)

A Man of Syn . . .

ASISTER acclaimed as England's leading dramatic actress is a hard act to follow. But if Russell never hit her theatrical heights he spread his wings wider, as actor, producer and author.

As very young children they played together in the shadowy vaults of Rochester Cathedral where their father was that seemingly denigrated ecclesiastical lesser-light, a Minor Canon, living in Minor Canons' Row. At five, Russell swapped Cathedral crypt for hen-coop 'study'. From there emanated jointly concocted plays such as 'The Dentist's Cure: Or Saw Their Silly Heads Off'. Village children were ruthlessly dragooned to support the two principals in drawing-room drama. Village children, for their father had been given the living at that loveliest of churches high above the Medway, at Aylesford.

Such theatricals pointed the way ahead. Sybil, after having renounced hopes of becoming a concert pianist when cramp, caused by over zealous practising, crippled her supple fingers, set her sights on the stage. Her first audition at Ben Greet's Acting Academy had to be cancelled because of a bilious attack (regarded by her Puritan father as Divine Judgement on a girl contemplating the infamy of life on the stage).

At the second attempt she was accepted - and so was Russell - thanks to her spirited advocacy. 'He's a far better actor than I am. Positively frightening. He makes your flesh creep'.. On the strength of this build-up Russell, obviously admirably equipped for Grand Guignol, joined the troupe, in 1904, for a four year long barn-storming tour of every state in America.

There, in Spartanburg, Grand Guignol became reality. As they rehearsed an idyllic scene from 'The Tempest', high in their tenement rooms, they heard a revolver shot . . . pounding feet . . . and cries of 'Murder!'. Below them a body lay bloodily sprawled on the sidewalk. A wife-beater had got his just deserts from a stepson who could no longer stomach his brutality.

After the tour Russell went on to make a name for himself as actor and producer in England. As Death, in 'Everyman', he received considerable acclaim but he never achieved his sister's eminence on the stage.

Later, a cheerful spendthrift, he was suddenly spurred by the indelible memory of that night to write, to bolster a tottering bank account. 'Master of the Macabre' - with its staring skull, bloodstained daggers, sexton's spade, and hanks of human hair - helped to make his name as an author.

It was a far cry too from Spartanburg to the one-time smugglers' village of Dymchurch on the Kent coast. There he'd spent boyhood holidays and played with Edith Nesbit's (q.v.) children. But the memory of the two-faced victim travelled with him. In 1915, Dr Syn was born. Ostensibly he was a respectable priest who cared for his flock as devotedly as sheep 'minders' on the nearby Marsh cared for theirs. By day, he penned hour-long sermons for his parishioners' Sabbath salvation. A zealous cleric indeed! But broadminded enough to enjoy a long pipe of Virginian tobacco and a drop of hot grog as he yarned with fishermen in the inn's snug.

By night, however, Christian pastor turned ruthless smuggler: respectable Dr Syn became feared 'Scarecrow'. That he would become a roaring success was unforeseen by Russell . . . Unwisely he killed off his goldmine character in the last chapter. Some years later, however, he skilfully resurrected him in six further smuggling yarns - based on Dr Syn's earlier life.

'The Scarecrow' took to the screen as well as the printed page with Whitstable's 'horror' actor, Peter Cushing, in the title role. With little head for money or for providence, Russell, it is said, exacted only a derisory £20 fee for the film rights. And splurged the lot in a glorious Chelsea pub binge with the boys!

Russell eventually returned to live permanently in Dymchurch. And in its inn to earn a reputation as a raconteur who certainly knew how to spin a yarn. Yarns of epic, almost Munchausen proportions . . . but they could have been true . . .

Quotation:
'He can roll his eyeballs like marbles'.
Sister and actress Sybil Thorndike

WALPOLE, Sir Hugh Seymour, CBE (1884-1941)

A Middlebrow Success . . .

Remarkably, his life story in its main essentials closely follows the same broad pattern of that of the friend he came to hate, Somerset Maugham.

Each was born abroad: Walpole in Auckland, New Zealand; Maugham in France. Each in early childhood was raised by a cleric: Walpole by his father who was to become Bishop of Edinburgh; Maugham by an austere Whitstable clergyman. Each came to England as a young child: Walpole at 5, Maugham at 10. Each was educated in Kent at King's School, Canterbury - where both were bullied. Each became bibliophile, art collector and wealthy novelist. And both showered the school where they had been so unhappy with munificent and unusual gifts.

Whilst Maugham plunged straight into life when leaving King's, Walpole went to Emmanuel College, Cambridge. From there, disillusioned by a spell in a Seamen's Mission, although intended for the Church, he tried his hand, unsuccessfully, as a teacher, at Epsom College. But at least the experience gave him the material for his first success, the ear-catching 'Mr Perrin and Mr Traill' (1911) - the story of the growing enmity and rivalry between old-fashioned Mr Perrin and young Mr Traill, full of new ideas totally alien to his colleague - and a rival for Amy Desart's hand!

Both 'The Dark Forest' and 'Secret City' were based on his service with the Red Cross in World War I with the Russian Ninth Army in Galicia and Petrograd. There - of all people - he met Somerset Maugham engaged on vital secret intelligence work. The latter book won Walpole the 1919 Tait Black Memorial Prize. 'The Man With Red Hair' was a venture into the macabre. 'Jeremy' and his Trollopean 'The Cathedral' smack of King's School, and Canterbury.

His best loved book is 'The Herries Chronicle' (1930-1933), a four-volume saga dramatically set in the Lake District. It was written there at Brackburn, his gloriously sited home at Manesty on the slopes of hump-backed Catbells (Home of the Wild Cat). From his study window he had an unforgettable view across Derwentwater to Falcon Crag and King's How . . . to Keswick lying under the bulk of Skiddaw . . . and to equally massive Blencathra.

'Borrowdale and Canterbury are the centre of my living - a little scrap of immortality that is all I shall have'. Yet he could stay at the former only a few weeks at a time before the siren call of London and his flat in Half

Moon Street called him irresistibly. Only there could he keep in the literary swim.

On one such London visit he was horrified to learn that Somerset Maugham, his friend for nearly two decades, had outrageously pilloried him in 'Cakes and Ale' (1930). Unmistakeably caricatured him for all eyes to read as Alroy Kear, a hypocritical literary opportunist both sycophantic and absurd! Walpole read it for himself in growing horror. Then hurried in ceaseless circles, like a dog with a tin can on its tail, round to his friends for comfort. 'He can't mean it?' pleaded a distraught Walpole. 'He can and he does' was Virginia Woolf's blunt reply.

Veiled jealousy probably lay behind so scurrilous an attack on a long-time friend. Walpole, for whose work Maugham had only conventional praise, was being promoted as the Grand Old Man of English Literature; had received a C.B.E. in 1917 for far less dangerous War Service than Maugham's; was urbane, tall and goodlooking where Maugham was small and was to become a parchment-faced 'mandarin'; spoke fluently without hint of the other's stammer or stutter.

Maugham wrote blandly (though he later admitted the charge) that in no way had he intended Kear to resemble him for he was merely a composite of many writers. Not entirely mollified, Walpole, when he replied, signed himself 'Alroy Maugham Walpole'.

Kear apart, Walpole worried, not unjustly, that he was old-fashioned, becoming left behind. And he envied the modernism of his friend and correspondent, Virginia Woolf. Her opinion of his work had a sting in its tail: 'Highly competent and smooth . . . moderately intelligent . . . but his art is sacrificed to facility . . . readable but never re-readable'. Walpole's pen undoubtedly had vivid descriptive power and an ability to evoke atmosphere which because of its very vividness was sometimes parodied.

It was Walpole's urbanity that attracted Virginia more than his writing. An urbanity once shattered when, seeking to visit her, he knocked at the wrong door . . . and was warmly greeted, not by Virginia but by a lady of a very different profession with richly carmined lips, generously hennaed hair, and an equally generous bosom of daunting proportions from whom, horrified, he disentangled himself only with great difficulty.

Time wiped out memories of being bullied but not of the beauties of King's School's medieval setting. 'I would be ready to wager' he asserted 'that no boy that lives for a number of years in the shadow of one of the loveliest Cathedrals in the world is likely to be unaffected'. And there too he maintained 'Character would never be flattened out into a colourless common denominator'.

In the 1920's, King's School had fallen on hard times. The newly appointed headmaster, Dr the Reverend F. J. Shirley, was a human dynamo. Walpole described him as 'an extraordinary man - has marvellour plans - but will have terrific rows'. How right he was! Caught in his spell, Walpole gave him all out support in his fight for a King's School renaissance.

He dipped his hand deep into his well-lined pockets for Shirley's regular appeals, and for the turfing of the Mint Yard, the School's focal point, where boys robbed of soccer kickabouts then had to play tamer stump-cricket. Gave too not only 'Deposition' in black Hopwood stone by Eric Gill (who remembered it as 'about the only carving of mine I'm not sorry about') but also his own portrait, painted - after he had shamelessly ditched Maugham's friend Gerald Kelly - by Augustus John; and a remarkable collection of MSS and old books from his Manesty library.

Generous in time as well as money, Walpole, in 1941, marched through Keswick in a Lakeland downpour on a War Savings Drive. Chilled and wet, he caught pneumonia and, despite the care and comfort of his friend and factotum (Walpole never drove), the former policeman Harold Cheevers, . . . died. He is buried in St John's churchyard in Keswick from where, one hopes, he can still see across the Lake and perhaps even down it to Manesty, Brackenburn . . . and the Herries Country.

Quotation:
'I have little doubt that he would have given all his popularity to gain the esteem of the intelligentsia. He knocked humbly at their doors and besought them to let him in, and it was a bitterness to him that they only laughed'.
Somerset Maugham, A Writer's Notebook

WALTON, Izaak (1593-1683)
Brother of the Angle . . .

IZAAK, the son of an ale-house keeper, had the comparative misfortune to be born in Staffordshire. But it was in Canterbury that he did his courting. And it was in Canterbury, in 1626, that, at St Mildred's-in-the-Castro Church, he married Rachell Floud, all of whose seven children were to die in infancy. She ranked high as a great-great-niece of Thomas Cranmer, who as a youth had married Black Joan of the Dolphin Tavern but still risen to become Archbishop of Canterbury.

And it was of Canterbury's River Stour at Fordwich that Izaak sang in highest praise of its trouts (sic), 'those rarest of fish'. Sang it in the most delightful book on angling ever written: 'The Compleat Angler or The Contemplative Man's Recreation'.

As to work, in 1618, he was sworn as a Free Brother of the select Ironmongers' Company. But from his 'half shop' in Fleet Street, London it was in the luxury trade of linen-draper that he prospered. Throve well enough to accumulate 'a modest competence which he exalted above riches'.

At St Dunstan's Church, his nearby and much revered neighbour was John Donne, adventurer, poet and priest. When he died it was Walton who mourned at his bedside, and it was Walton who insisted on writing his biography to make complete a collection of sermons. This was the first of three lives he wrote celebrating Kentish friends: Donne of Sevenoaks; Sir Henry Wotton of Boughton Malherbe, and Richard Hooker of Bishopsbourne.

With such a close friend as the 'divine Donne', it is hardly surprising that Izaak loved poetry, dabbled in it himself, but stoutly averred 'I am not excellent at poetry'. It is his prose, his 'Compleat Angler', that has stood the test of time. A glorious hotchpotch: a genial book of instruction spiced with fishy fables and fancies; poems and anecdotes; even occasional moral digressions. Full of friendliness and the joy of living, it is subtitled 'A Discourse on Rivers, Fish-ponds, Fish and Fishing'; and it is written in dialogue between Piscator (Walton); Venerata (a hunter); and Auceps (a falconer): two complete strangers he had greeted on the river bank and eagerly introduced to angling.

Each freshwater fish from Pike, the Tyrant of the River, to Tench, the Physician of Fishes, is described in loving detail - less lovingly though, how to bring about its downfall. The beliefs of his day too: . . . the eel is frightened by thunder; an otter can hear a fish stir 40 furlongs away; a frog which keeps its mouth closed all winter; the restless palmer worm that boldly and disorderly will wander up and down and cannot endure to be kept to an habitual diet; bait anointed with the marrow of a heron's thigh bone is an irresistible temptation; the faithfulness to death of the female mullet:

'As mad with woe to shore she followeth
Prest to consort him both in life and death'.

He quotes knowledgeably from Martial, Lucian and Pliny. Even from Prague's Bishop Thurzo who stoutly maintained that he had seen a frog leap onto a pike's back and claw out its eyes. 'A tale', said the sceptics, 'as likely as a mouse scratching out the eyes of a cat'.

With the sun beginning to sink he and his companions would head happily for a riverside inn to drink Red Cows' milk, good ale; play shovelboard; and be as happy to sing a song themselves as to listen to one sweetly sung by a pretty milkmaid. To dine well too for Izaak would discourse as enthusiastically on 'a Brave Breakfast of Powdered Beef and a Radish or Two' as on the preparation of a carp, a yard long, with Sweet Marjoram and Winter Savory, oysters and anchovies, a pound of sweet butter, a sauce of orange juice and garlic - and the whole basted in claret. It was a dish 'too good for any but anglers or very honest men'.

He quoted delightedly from the poets of his age, Marlowe and Drayton, Sir Henry Wotton and the Divine Dubartas, and from Donne's neat plagiarisation of Marlowe's famous verse:

'Come live with me and be my love
And we will new pleasures prove
Of golden sands and crystal brooks
With silken lines and silver hooks'.

Fordwich trout, which took the bait, not from hunger but from sheer wantonness, ranked high in his esteem because they 'grew to the bigness of a salmon'. It was a fish, he maintained, that knew almost to a day when to leave the salt sea for the dangers of the Stour's freshwater. Unfortunately for the trout - so did the Townsmen. Canterbury Museum boasts such a specimen, one taken in 1672, and weighing a phenomenal 27 lb.

Dr Johnson praised the ease and unaffected humour of the dialogue; Sir Walter Scott rhapsodised on the beautiful simplicity of his Arcadian prose; and even Wordsworth hailed him as 'Sage Benign'. Not surprisingly his brother-in-law went so far as to compare his book with the famous Colloquies of Erasmus.

No less unsurprising was the complaint of blunt Cromwellian Roundhead trooper, Richard Franck: 'Walton stuffs his indigested octavo with other men's observations'. Not surprising because the little Fleet Street linen-draper, a staunch Royalist, had been courageous enough to help smuggle back to Charles II the Garter Regalia which had been abandoned in the flight from the battlefield of Worcester. And 'mad, bad and dangerous to know' Lord Byron, who, however, was hardly gentle with his women, wrote:

'Whatever Izaac Walton sings or says,
The quaint old cruel coxcomb in his gullet
Should have a hook, and a small trout to pull it'.

Walton may have been 'a man of low situation in life' but he was familiar with many great men. He passed his later years with his boon companion of 40 years standing, George Morley, Bishop of Winchester, and was buried there in the Cathedral.

Quotation:
'Of this just man, let his just praise be given:
Heaven was in him, before he was in Heaven.
Dr Richard Sibbes

WEIL, Simone (1903-1943)

Philosopher, Mystic or Saint . . . ?

A JEWESS, descended from a long line of agnostic intellectuals, she was born and brought up in Paris - but died in Kent. Educated at a school for gifted boys - at the Lycée Henri VI - and at the prestigious École Normale Superieure (which invariably turned its sexist nose up at the mere mention of women). She read Literature, Philosophy and Logic: passing all with meteoric brilliance. Not entirely surprising when you know that her brother André, three years her senior, was already tipped to be 'Mathematician of the Century'!

For all this, Simone was an odd fish. Her lecturers feared that her ceaseless quest for originality was verging perilously close on eccentricity. Not for nothing did they label her 'The categoric in skirts'.

Her fellow students found her distant, unapproachable. And in politics they called her the 'Red Virgin' for she flirted dangerously with Bolshevism. But in the end she could never bring herself to take the plunge into either organised politics or religion.

But then what *do* you make of a young woman who, as a child, always pleaded, even blackmailed, for the most unpleasant of the household chores; who already had the moral intensity of a mature woman; who, at three, spurned gifts, money, luxury. Even now she still has something of the family obsession about almost ceaseless washing; about bodily contact - especially kissing, a certain carrier of disease!

Graduating, in 1931, the shooting star plummetted down to earth, to teach in a girls' school at Le Puy. But then, even the most liberal of headmasters tends to be shocked when he finds one of his young staff vehemently haranguing a strikers' apathetic demonstration - directly outside the school at that! Simone had to go.

Go she did: to two other schools, to agriculture, and to industry. In between teaching posts she quit the rarified atmosphere of scholarship to find out for herself how *real* people really worked and lived and died. She turned to industry to work a power-press amid the dirt and din of the Renault factory. 'After that', she said, 'I always bore the mark of a slave'. She turned too to farming: to demand, even in the bleakest weather, the roughest and the toughest of labouring tasks - almost as her right.

Simone learnt how 'the poor and powerless, the oppressed and the exploited' lived. And then she devoted her life tirelessly to fight their battles.

In 1938 she made her way to Spain as a non-belligerent to help its oppressed and exploited workers in their one-sided fight against Generalissimo Franco. 1941 found her in Marseilles sitting at the feet of Dominican Father Perrin. But a year later she fled her country, fled Occupied France for America - but only because otherwise her ageing parents would never have gone to safety without her.

Within six months she was back in Europe. In England, at Free French H.Q. in London. There she sowed the seeds of her own death, working all hours, and refusing to eat even as much as the meagre rations of her countrymen under German domination. So too, she had refused to heat her room when she worked at Renault because she found that the poor could not afford to do the same.

In 1938 Simone had had a mystical experience - of being one with Christ and His love. She leant towards Catholicism but eventually would have nothing of organised religion. Her books 'Attente de Dieu' ('Waiting on God') and 'Gateway to God' were not published until some years after her death.

It was a death from tuberculosis. One exacerbated by her Spartan life, by her refusal to eat enough. A death that occurred not in Paris or London but in the little known town of Ashford in Kent, at the Grosvenor Sanatorium. There after one brief week she died. Died to force a world at war's attention to her 'poor and oppressed' - the 7,000,000 refugees it had created.

Today she lies nearby in Bybrook Cemetery, unknown, unnoticed. But her name is still honoured in Ashford in pleasantly landscaped Simone Weil Way.

Quotation:
'A test of what is real is that it is hard and rough. Joys are found in it, not pleasure. What is pleasant belongs to dreams'.
Simone Weil

WELLS, Herbert George (1866-1946)

Volatile Visionary . . .

THE man whose vast and varied output of books made him England's leading literary figure for 40 years was born at Bromley ('a suburb of the damnedest'). He was the son of a failed shopkeeper, a man of benign irresponsibility - but a successful Kent County cricketer who once achieved the staggering figures of 4 wickets in 4 balls - all clean bowled! His mother was a lady's maid. As only death or bankruptcy was likely to part them from a sadly ailing china shop at 47 High Street, both had to work.

H.G.'s early days were, educationally, as varied as his books were to be: dame school, village school, Commercial Academy, Midhurst Grammar School - interspersed with two spells, when money was short, 'in the drapery', made desperately miserable by petty tyrannies and humiliations, long hours and minimal pay.

His mother, to make ends meet, worked at palatial Uppark where servants, preferably, were to be neither seen nor heard. She insisted he spent his holidays with her there so that he might cling to the coat-tails of gentility, and have books enough to satisfy his voracious appetite. He prepared too for his later amorous life - by successfully chasing not unwilling tweenies.

In 1884, he fought his Scholarship way into today's Imperial College of Science. There he was inspired by the famous biologist T. H. Huxley but 'behaved like a detestable hobbledehoy to other lecturers'. Despite that, he emerged, in 1890, a Batchelor of Science with First Class Honours, to teach, amongst others, the famous newspaper magnate to be, Lord Northcliffe (qv).

All too hastily he plunged into marriage with his cousin, Isabel (1891). Within two years her inability to respond fiercely enough to him sexually, drove him into the arms of a student, Catherine ('Jane') Robbins. She was to turn the benignest and blindest of eyes to his later numerous infidelities, and to support him loyally and lovingly until her death from cancer, during which he nursed her with all his old love.

Shortly after their marriage, whilst on a South Coast cycling tour, a malfunctioning kidney left him under the threat of the knife had it not 'practically taken itself off' - and left nothing for removal! Warned by his doctor to live in dry air, on dry subsoil, he perversely moved to Beach Cottage at Sandgate, near Folkestone - where riotous south-easters crash down and hurl spray and shingle clean over the roofs.

There, successful with his short stories, he found new life, new ideas, and a new commercial toughness that 'was altogether ungenteel'. As a result he could afford to employ a leading architect, C. F. A. Voysey, to design Spade House for him high above, on Folkestone's Leas. It stood near the old hydraulic lift whose attendants, mistaking him for Joseph Hobson Jagger, 'The Man Who Broke The Bank At Monte Carlo' with 2,000,000 frames won in eight days, told awestruck tourists, 'All on the turn of that ace of spades!'

Superbly housed and happily married, he nevertheless became a self-chartered libertine. He transmuted Ella D'Arcy's kindliness into passion; made love to soulful, and deliciously dimpled, Dorothy Richardson in the bracken between Eridge and Frant; had a steamy jungle episode with an insatiable Amber Reeves who had a 'sharp, Levantine face, a nimble body . . . and as little discretion as a Town Crier'.

He even entered into aristocratic relations with Countess Elizabeth Russell; and international ones with Moura Budberg the magnificent, Gorky's mistress, Odette Keun, and Frau Hedwig Gatternigg who dramatically cut her throat (not too seriously!) when finally rejected as no longer of interest. Jane, slightly perturbed, but in no way rancorous, suggested they moved to London, where they could both indulge their very different tastes.

This was only the starting gun for a stormy ten-year clandestine affaire - but it was a joining of minds as well as of bodies. It started when Rebecca West, a 19 year old cub reporter of 'Freewoman', 26 years his junior, derided the great H. G. Wells' efforts to write of passion in his novel 'Marriage'. 'Your efforts are like cold white sauce; you are the Old Maid of novelists'. Hardly likely to endear her to a man proud of his reputation as a seducer. But it did - he fell for her sharp mind as much as for her dark and striking appearance: *une brune adorable.*

When convention forced them even briefly apart Jaguar wrote (some 800 letters - often childishly, humorously illustrated) to his Panther. 'There is NO Panfer but Panfer and she is the Prophet of the Most High Jaguar which is Bliss and Perfect Being'. For all such extravagant endearments there were jagged rocks ahead - largely because of Wells' selfishness and ill-temper and his failure to recognise *her* literary genius.

When, after ten years, the once passionate affaire gradually petered out, Rebecca, now free of restraint, showed she could stand almost as high as Wells: eight novels; a brilliant analysis of World War II origins in 'Black Lamb and Grey Falcon'; organisation of BBC wartime broadcasts to Yugoslavia; her reportage of the Nuremberg Trials, and a fling with Lord Beaverbrook. 'She wrote as brilliantly as ever I could - and much more savagely' wrote G.B.S. High praise indeed!

Wells' literary range was as fantastic as his own highly popular fantasy stories, which were probably his best work. 'War of the Worlds' (1898) and 'First Men on the Moon' (1901) were years ahead of their time.

'The Time Machine' shoots its readers forward into the year 802701: into the midst of the epicene flower-people, the Eloi, 'beautifully futile' by day - terrified when on moonless nights the man-eaters, the Morlocks, emerge from the depths. And on until the world was 'an abominable desolation,' peopled only by huge white butterflies and malign crabs as big as tables. 'The Island of Dr Moreau' was the most horrifying of all with the creation of man-animals; and was an attack on unethical experiments of his day which are rearing their heads even now.

Completely different, equally brilliant, were his comedies. Mr Polly, the failure and dismal drifter, by sheer hilarious chance, becomes a hero, seeks a new life, and by standing firm against psychopath Uncle Jim, at last achieves success and contentment at the idyllic Potwell Inn. 'Kipps' was the story of a young drapery assistant. ('We're in a blessed drainpipe and must crawl along it until we die'.) He comes into money, seeks middle-class status, is cheated out of his windfall, and finds real happiness only when he returns to his first love. It has all the salty tang of New Romney, Hythe and Folkestone, and of Wells' own misery 'in the drapery'.

The eponymous 'Anna Veronica' sought to break away from the confining bonds of traditional feminism . . . and the book was branded 'literary filth', 'this poisonous book' and 'a community of scuffling stoats and ferrets'. Sociological 'Utopia' pointed the way to 'a fairer shares for all the world'. His 'Short History of the World' made no mention of Shakespeare, and crisply dismissed Christ in a single page. 'Work, Wealth and Happiness of Mankind' was a best seller his 'Experiment in Autobiography' something of a *tour de force* revealing not only the true Wells but also the literary figures of his day, Thomas Hardy, John Galsworthy, Bertrand Russell . . .

The whole world became his oyster: he toured Russia and an adulatory America; interviewed Stalin and Lenin as well as Roosevelt; and continued to turn out a ceaseless flow of short stories, pamphlets, tracts, articles and commentaries. 114 major works was his incredible tally!

Quotation:
'You delighted us, excited and angered us. You offered us all the world in tempting cans with lively labels: Free Love; Education; World Organisation; and Marriage'.
Freda Kirchwey

WOTTON, Sir Henry (1568-1639)

Ambassador extraordinary . . .

AS befitting a young man with a family tree dating as far back as Sherwood Forest's Major Oak, with a Winchester-Oxford background, he had the world at his feet as he set out on a seven-year Grand Tour.

On his return, the Earl of Essex, no less, sent him again into a turbulent Europe as his under-cover agent (1595). There he was to scent any hint of assassination attempts planned against Essex' beloved Queen. For Wotton it was all a very different world from the Wealden quiet that enveloped his splendid Tudor brick mansion at Boughton Malherbe. He found that the Italians in general were 'an amalgam of politeness - and perfidy'; Florence was 'a Paradise - inhabited by devils'; Rome, 'the centre of corruption'.

He returned with no recognition of his abilities as a 16th century sleuth. But he did come back with an abiding love of the art and architecture of Italy. So polished a courtier was he now that 'to converse with him was one of the delights of mankind'.

From under-cover agent to full-blooded adventurer. He sailed with Essex in the Ark Royal to Cadiz . . . and on a less profitable sally to the Azores. He sailed with him too, much less successfully, to Ireland where Hugh O'Neill forced a humiliating peace (1601). Wisely, he left Essex to face Elizabeth's outraged wrath - and stole quietly back to the Continent.

Not so quietly though for his host, Ferdinand, Duke of Tuscany, had unearthed a plot against, not Elizabeth, but her heavily tipped successor-to-be, James VI of Scotland. And Ferdinand needed a discreet and trustworthy messenger to carry such a vital warning to Scotland. So Henry became 'Ottavio Baldi' and with Ducal letters and, melodramatically, a casket of antidotes for poison, he galloped back across Europe.

Not ungrateful, James on his succession as James I of England, rewarded him: plain Henry Wotton of Boughton Malherbe became *Sir* Henry Wotton, Ambassador to the Doge of Venice (1604). Seven idyllic years there: to revel in the rich mosaics of St Mark's, the austerity of great bare brick churches, and the Byzantine palaces.   ˙

Then the storm broke about his unwitting head. Seven years before, in a friend's album, he had jestingly penned the aphorism: 'An Ambassador is an honest man sent to lie abroad for his country'. 'Lie' was a harmless, jesting *double entendre* for English readers . . . Not so, however, for a malicious Italian Romanist, Gaspar Scoppius, who all too delightedly published it abroad. If mere ambassadors lied, then what of their kings . . . ?

James was not amused! In desperation Sir Henry had earnest disclaimers scattered as lavishly over Europe as today's advertising touts scatter handouts in the High Street. So 'choicely eloquent' were they however that grudgingly he was forgiven by his sorely tried monarch. And allowed to find a peaceful anonymity as Provost of Eton. To be a man 'who loves to do little'. To angle at leisure with his friend and quirky biographer, Sir Izaak Walton.

Sir Henry was of course as facile with pen as with rod:

'How happy to be born and taught,
That serveth not another's will;
Whose armour is his honest thought,
And simple Truth his utmost skill'.

Lovelier still was 'On His Mistress, the Queen of Bohemia':

'You meaner beauties of the Night . . .
What are you when the Sun shall rise?'.

Quotation:
'He first deceased; she for a little tried
to live without him, liked it not, and died'.
Epitaph for friends by Sir Henry Wotton

WYATT, Sir Thomas, The Elder (1503-1542)

The Best Poet of his Age . . .

HE was born beside the peaceful reaches of the Medway at Allington Castle, 'where is spoke as brode and rude English as anywhere in Kent'. Nevertheless, he was to become a poet of great delicacy. And he was as nearly to lose his head as his son, Thomas the Younger, actually did when he rashly raised Kent against Queen Mary's Spanish marriage.

When time allowed, particularly in later life, he always returned to Allington.

'This maketh me at home to hunt and hawk
And in foul weather at my book to sit . . .
For here I am in Kent and Christendom'.

As a boy he reared within the castle walls a lion cub which one day would have savaged him but for the timely intervention of his favourite greyhound. It was a cat - not a dog - which next saved his life, when he

96

was half starved and frozen to the marrow in the gnawing cold of the Tower, by thrusting through the bars of his cell fresh-killed pigeons.

His parents were fearless. His father had fought against all Henry VII's enemies: Scots, French and rebels alike. And his mother had not hesitated to set in the stocks one who had been 'wantonly playing pranks' with her serving maids - her neighbour, the Abbot of Boxley!

Thomas was a man's man, a giant in the joust, a gallant at Court. He rose steadily in Royal favour: Treasurer of the King's Jewels; courtier at the Field of the Cloth of Gold; diplomatic emissary to Venice and to the Pope. In the latter role he was captured by Spanish troops, imprisoned, ransomed - and escaped with the messenger bearing the 3,000 ducats for his release. If that was not sufficient he became Marshal of Calais; Esquire of the Royal Body; Chief Ewerer at Ann Boleyn's sumptuous coronation feast; High Sheriff of the Abbey at Malling; Commander of all men 'able for war' in the seven Hundreds of Kent; a Knight on Easter Day 1535 - and a very temporary resident of the Fleet Prison after he had committed the trifling offence of killing a night Guard.

Such royal favour might never have been his when, at Court, he fell for the eloquent black eyes of a Kentish girl: eyes that even at 14 had 'enthralled many gentlemen'. In the manner of the period he courted her with passionate and flattering verses, one of which is inscribed 'I ama yowres' (Love, Anne). And it was her vivacity in conversation 'wherein he had singular delight' that drove him to write 'I could gladly be tied for ever with the knot of her love'.

But shortly Henry VIII's lecherous eyes were on her, on Anne Boleyn, the woman destined 'to set all England in a roar'. When a peevish Henry claimed 'the head' at bowls, Thomas deliberately took its measure with a love token he had snatched from her. Furiously jabbing an admonitory finger encircled by Anne's ring, the King stormed 'Wait, I tell thee it is mine - or I am deceived'. According however to a dubious source, one Nicholas Sander, Wyatt as a known suitor of the girl to be Queen, had preferred to risk present rather than future trouble.

He daringly warned the King of the unsuitability of his proposed match, 'She is not meet to be coupled with Your Grace; her conversation is loose and base - she has allowed me carnal knowledge'. Amazingly, love-blinded Henry merely derided him but left him in fear, years later, when the object of the King's eternal love was 'on trial' for immorality that he too might be named with the four luckless and probably innocent accused - and share their fate of the rack and execution.

Lucky Thomas got away with it - and lived to write still more poetry. He was a versatile and innovative poet, simple and direct, using short but varied lines. Yet, strangely, nearly all his verses were full of melancholy and self-pity. For him Love was always a Paradise Lost of passionate and sustained unhappiness.

'They flee from me that sometime did me seek
With naked foot stalking in my chamber'.

Even music held no more charm for him:

'My lute be still for I have done'.

His bitter 'Satires' and 'Penitential Psalms' showed his violent disgust at statesmen's broken promises and courtiers' corruption:

'. . . for swine so groan
In sty, and chaw the turds moulded on the ground,
And drivel on pearls; the head still in the manger,
Than of the harp the ass to hear the sound'.

He inveighs even against 'Fortune, I have found thee unjust'.

In 1542, restored to Royal favour, he was dispatched to Falmouth to welcome the ambassador of the Holy Roman Emperor Charles V. Riding post-haste day and night, and heedless of foul weather, he was so exhausted that he had to rein in at Sherborne - and dying there never remounted.

Quotation:
'A kind and faithful public servant in a hard-hearted and
faithless Court'.
G. M. Trevelyan